THE MOONLIT GARDEN

The
MOONLIT
GARDEN

Writings by Scott Ogden

TAYLOR PUBLISHING COMPANY
Dallas, Texas

Published by Taylor Publishing Company
1550 West Mockingbird Lane
Dallas, Texas 75235

Library of Congress Cataloging-in-Publication Data

Ogden, Scott.
The moonlit garden / writings by Scott Ogden.
p.   cm.
Includes bibliographical references and index.
ISBN 0-87833-893-4
1. Night gardens. 2. Night-flowering plants.
3. Night-fragrant flowers. I. Title.
SB433.6.O44   1998
635.9'53—dc21   98–10604
CIP

Printed in the United States of America

10 9 8 7 6 5 4 3 2 1

For Adam and Sarah

CONTENTS

PREFACE

If a garden does what it is supposed to do, it becomes for the gardener a territory filled with magic and mystery. To walk in it is to be engaged and distracted, seduced, and eventually, consumed. The ongoing relationship of a human being with a certain plot of ground is at its heart a romance, for to garden honestly is to fall in love, in love with the rhythms and miracles of nature, in love with life itself.

The reality of this affection is nowhere clearer than in a darkened garden tenderly illuminated by moonbeams. In the half light, we discover ourselves and the very essence of our experience. Such frankly romantic feelings toward the garden at night have been voiced since pleasure grounds were first created.

What I hope to share in this book is my fascination with the moonlit garden, with its vegetal and animal inhabitants, its reflective stones and minerals, and its nocturnal regent, the moon. My perspective and experience and my own enchantment with this subject have been realized mostly in Texas, but the observations in this book will serve gardeners in the South and Southwest as well as, in a more general way, across the country.

ACKNOWLEDGMENTS

For assistance, support, and inspiration, I offer thanks to Larry DeMartino, Doris Martin, Jane Schweppe, Anne Ashmun, Grady Taylor, Dan Hosage Jr., Paul Cox, Greg Grant, my family, and the others whose love of gardens and nature has touched my life.

Already with thee! tender is the night,
And haply the Queen-Moon is on her throne,
Clustered around by all her starry Fays;
But here there is no light,
Save what from heaven is with the breezes blown
Through verdurous glooms and winding mossy ways

I cannot see what flowers are at my feet,
Nor what soft incense hangs upon the boughs,
But, in embalmèd darkness, guess each sweet
Wherewith the seasonable month endows
The grass, the thicket, and the fruit tree wild;
White hawthorn, and the pastoral eglantine;
Fast fading violets covered up in leaves;
And mid-May's eldest child,
The coming musk rose, full of dewy wine,
The murmurous haunt of flies on summer eves.

JOHN KEATS, FROM ODE TO A NIGHTINGALE

INTRODUCTION

The Moon Garden

he light of the moon falls upon a magnificent kingdom, yet it is a realm revealed to a fortunate few. Ordinary gardeners shy from the nocturnal universe, neglecting their leafy charges at the first sign of dusk. This is a foolish decision, for the floral community remains vast and willing. The blossoms of darkness stand ready to endow gardens with intimate beauty and precious fragrance. Although pallid, the flowers of the moon's kingdom engage us with potency, as a lover's whisper reaches the heart with greater force than a shout.

If truth be told, the most glorious garden by day seems static and spiritless compared to its nocturnal counterpart. Even with the bright colors of sunlight, fully illuminated grounds present a flat, two-dimensional veneer. Moonlight imparts a muted depth and callow sensuality. The velvety luminescence paints over disparate elements; the scene dissolves into a harmonious whole.

Walls and hedges and views of neighboring houses and trees all recede mysteriously into blackness. In the gentle pallor of the moon familiar, compartmentalized surroundings transform into ethereal places of uncertain distance and unknown purpose.

As evening approaches, sunlight fades and leaves in its place a feeling of heightened awareness. Witnesses to the demise of the day call more by more upon neglected senses of hearing, smell, and touch. Dictatorial sight steps down to a modest office as the sun abdicates dominion over the garden.

The last, dying rays ignite an electric fluorescence, signaling transfer of power to the moon and her court of glittering stars. Like the gentle illumination of a Vermeer painting, the land glows even as the light of the sky fades. The whole garden takes on the blended hues of summer in the Arctic.

A momentary sense of foreboding accompanies the fading light, as if a chill breeze had passed or a shadowy phantom had entered the garden. Uneasiness at the death of the day soon lapses to fascination with the moon's dark kingdom.

Reassurance comes in the trill, chirping voices of crickets and cicadas welcoming the evening. Their rhythmic, hypnotic songs establish a steady, confident concert, soon joined by the merry ratcheting and percussive barking of katydids and tree frogs. In the air above, barely discerned silhouettes of bats and night hawks confirm the gentle sounds of flapping wings. In the garden itself, whirrings and bustlings of busy hawkmoths signal the evening round of nectar gathering.

Silver leaves, pale stones, and gravely pathways suffuse with an eerie glow. Dark columns built of thick trees and dense shrubberies rise up to support the celestial firmament. Through the borders, ivory blossoms expand and glisten in the pale light.

Darkness descends in earnest, and observers feel the gentle, gravid strokes of the evening winds. Cooling dew settles over all. Like a potent hallucinogen, the pregnant atmosphere breathes a succession of olfactory visions: freshly mown hay piles; mouldering logs; thick-tangled honeysuckles; ancient, spicy damask roses; smoky pungent artemisias. These appear to the mind's eye with more brilliant illumination than was ever provided by the sun.

The moon garden offers a temple to the senses. Like the blind, the witness to the nocturnal landscape learns more immediate ways to connect with his surroundings. Voids in perception left by the departing light fill with myriad sounds and fragrances as the keen, cool touch of the evening air keeps the mind marvelously alert. In a wondrous paradox, experience of the garden heightens as it fades from view.

That moon and stars are the rightful regents of gardens was once common wisdom, for the moon figures prominently in the horticultural traditions of nearly all the earth's cultures. The rhythm of the moon-driven tides echoes in our very heartbeats, even as the monthly reproductive cycle of women verifies the moon's mystic power over life on earth.

Throughout the year and in limitless settings and aspects, the light of the moon casts its spell over gardens. The spiritual alchemy that follows remains available to all who will pause and allow it into their hearts. In that pale illumination, we come to know the gentle gladness of nature as we make friends with the night and its inhabitants.

*Perhaps it will seem contrary to begin the garden
year with winter, but to me it begins with the flowering of the first paper-whites and sweet violets after
heavy frost has cut down the last chrysanthemum.
We do not have to wait for spring to start the new
season. After the slimy stalks of fall flowers have
been cleared away, the garden assumes its winter
aspect, and winter flowers begin to bloom.*

ELIZABETH LAWRENCE, A SOUTHERN GARDEN

ONE

Winter Fragrances

hen a gardener has become thoroughly settled and comfortable with the colors and scents of summer days, it is time to
go wandering in winter night.

If a person has a strong affinity for plants, there comes a
moment when the daisies and roses identify themselves sim-
ply by the feel of their leaves. Even with eyes closed, gently crushed petals and
foliage reveal fragrances that can be recognized. By the time we know when to
expect the yellow lilies and which handsome, feather-leaved herbs may be
planted to flower alongside, our easy familiarity needs to be uprooted and reset
in mysterious, frigid grounds.

On those clear, chill evenings when winter moons dispel the icy clouds,
a forbidding iridescence diffuses over the land. In the void Orion and the
Pleiades sparkle and add their distant brilliance. Frost falls, and crystalline
traceries materialize along the edges of withered leaves and crisp stems, the
spent abundance of last summer.

The frozen moonlight discloses naked, lifeless branches and austere,
empty places, revealing nature in her demise. Everywhere the skeletal under-
pinnings of the land, its paths and ledges, tree trunks and stones, open glades
and tidy allees, show themselves in clarity. If the garden has been well
planned, its underlying goodness is as strong as ever, and there is a sense of
beauty even in this oblivion, but this is not a place to linger.

For plants and gardeners better times come when winter skies fill with
gray and night mantles in dampness. Although bleak, the clouded heavens

enclose plantings like a blanket. This cold embrace offers sufficient warmth to ward off frost and provides a dewy, vapor-filled atmosphere to convey the fragrances of evening blooms.

Most gardeners know some winter flowers, but few suspect the variety that may be enlisted for night-time plantings. Often, there are shrubs and early bulbs that offer blooms when the weather warms. While most of the herbaceous layer of the garden sleeps, these plants carry the season.

Winter flowers are visited by a surprising array of insects. These include honeybees and small bees like the mining bee, sweat bee, and mason bee, the long-tongued bee-flies and flower flies, and night-flying moths of hardy genera that possess a sort of natural antifreeze used to help survive cold weather. These are joined, inevitably, by certain beetles and by the clouded sulfur, that small yellow butterfly who "puts a finger in everyone's pie." During periods of hard frost, the insects shelter under fallen leaves. When a moment of false spring arrives, as may happen anytime from November onward, they emerge to feed among flowers that rise to the same capricious opportunities.

Shining Flowers of Winter

Some of the first nocturnal blossoms of the frost appear on large, exotic shrubs from the temperate forests of China. Their botanical name, *Chimonanthus nitens*, translates as "shining flower of winter." Although not common in gardens, they might be planted more, as the mounding stems develop into sturdy, spreading masses cloaked with stiff evergreen leaves.

Ghostly, transparent blooms drape along the sprawling branches from October into the new year. These odd flowers look like slivers of rice paper dangled from the twigs; at night they glow against the dark, pointed foliage and emanate a light, peculiar fragrance. Who would imagine that, as much as anything, this odor recalls the scent of embalming fluid? Although not particularly pleasant, this seems appropriate to a flower that begins its season at Halloween.

A better-known cousin, the wintersweet (*Chimonanthus praecox*) offers a more delectable perfume, although it grows as a brutishly large, ungraceful shrub. Most of its heavy-textured leaves shed before peak flowering in January; first blooms arrive as early as Thanksgiving; the last may linger into March.

Small bowls that seem to be fashioned of beeswax open through several weeks from tight buds scattered up and down the twigs. The little blooms mimic tiny coppery waterlilies, a witness to this shrub's primitive affinity with the ancient family of magnolias. The yellowish sepals enclose maroon-stained ranks of petals, which cup together and radiate a penetrating fragrance like spiced honey. This heady, sweet aroma carries for yards when evenings are mild and slightly damp.

Like many oriental shrubs, *Chimonanthus* tolerate soil and climate extremes and adapt to both sun and shade. They are a delight in gardens large enough to house their sprawling ten-foot bulk. The thin-textured, fragrant blooms offer an ethereal backdrop to wintry borders and might serve as hedges to enclose a moonlit terrace. 'Lutea,' a selection of wintersweet with especially translucent all-yellow blossoms, is a good variety for plantings that will be visited in darkness.

Witching Wood

When the world is green and growing, a dim woodland path is a secret place where fairies dance and lovers meet; in winter it's where witch hazels fulfill occult rituals of bloom. In nature, these small, crooked trees seek deep, humusy soils and protected woodland dells. This is where these curious plants seem most at home in gardens, too, although the common American witch hazel (*Hamamelis virginiana*), is tough enough to thrive in open prairie.

Colonists favored the pliant, gently spiraled branches for water-witching, or dousing, and this is the supposed origin of the shrub's common name. Four long, twisted petals join in a small cup to form the fragrant flowers, which have a strangely crumpled, crapelike appearance. As a fascinating adaptation, these spidery blossoms roll up on cold days for protection against frost. If pollination succeeds, the blooms develop into woody capsules. These open explosively during the sunny days of Indian Summer, spitting nutlike seeds several feet through the air.

About the first week of November, just as foliage begins to yellow and drop, *H. virginiana* begins a modest two-week display of feathery, lemon-tinted threads along twisted, upright branches. These tiny blooms form a delicate frostlike tracery in the gloomy light of dusk or when backlit by the moon.

The other North American witch hazel, *Hamamelis vernalis*, stirs at midwinter to flower for several weeks. The reddish calyx, or cup, of this species holds petals that vary from gold to copper or rust. 'Carnea' is particularly deep colored. All forms emit a pungent, spicy-sweet fragrance that carries on winter air and may be enjoyed on dark nights when the flowers cannot be seen. *H. vernalis* does well on damp soils and has proven adaptable to difficult urban situations. In the South, it grows as a native of swampy woodland.

Although not so forgiving, the Chinese and Japanese witch hazels provide ribbony blossoms up to two inches in diameter. The lemon-toned *H. x intermedia* 'Arnold Promise' and the lighter yellow 'Pallida' are especially fine garden forms worth sheltered nooks in the winter garden. Their ravishingly fragrant sulfury blooms unfold from furry brown buds during January and continue to scent the air for weeks. A little moonlight causes them to glow against the dismal carpet of leaves in the quiet of a winter wood.

Sweet Frost

Despite endearing fragrance and old-fashioned charm, winter honeysuckle (*Lonicera fragrantissima*) has lost many of its admirers, for it commits the modern sin of growing to estate size. There is nothing flashy or bright about the bush, either. Most of the year it simply presents an arching mass of drab, rounded gray-green foliage ten-feet high and nearly as wide.

Yet, as if a beneficent blizzard coated each branch, tiny pairs of sweet-scented blooms line the pliant stems every January. These crumpled blossoms, transparent as ice, display the same parchment quality as witch hazels and, like them, unfold from tight buds between bouts of frost. The unassuming flowers dispense a fragrance that calls to mind magnolias and jasmines. Few gardeners who have inhaled this illusion of summer would be without it by choice.

In the South, bush honeysuckles retain some of their leaves through winter, although this tardy foliage is usually half yellowed. At night, the mixture of disheveled gray and gold shows happily through gloom, so that these otherwise graceless shrubs become assets, both visual and olfactory. When it is realized that the plants accept poor soils and harsh exposures, their value becomes obvious. Rows of them would make a marvelous nighttime allee to frame a grand winter border.

Cinnamon at Christmas

As the solstice approaches, the lengthening nights fill with perfume like some sweetened spice. This pleasant, sugary aroma brings to mind the cinnamon sticks swizzled in holiday mugs of chocolate or cider. A search through winter shadows for its source eventually leads back to large, dark-foliaged evergreens.

The light of dawn reveals the Japanese plum, or loquat (*Eriobotrya japonica*), a ubiquitous, leafy shrub of the South, popular for fast screens and hedges. Though typical of vulgar plantings around apartment complexes, tourist courts, and industrial offices, the subtropical loquats have much to endear them in more personal surroundings.

The handsome leaves give good service and offer useful contrasts to light-colored stones and foliage. The marvelous confectionery fragrance, although evident in the evening, is a daytime scent as well. Bees may be seen furiously working the blossoms on mild winter afternoons. After pollination, the clusters of smallish, five-petaled blooms swell to become groups of tart orange-yellow fruits. These small orbs hang from the branches in late spring, offering feasts for migrating cedar waxwings.

With their easy growth and tolerance of drought, loquats provide practical additions for gardens not subject to undue frost. Although they may be damaged in unusually cold seasons, the trees can be counted hardy near the gulf and will add their crisp, sweet scent to evenings well north of this if planted near a wall.

À la Belle Étoile

In the cloistered gardens of old New Orleans, the mild air of winter fills with another mysterious aroma, one like spiced oranges. This famous fragrance drifts outwards from the thickset branches of sweet olive (*Osmanthus fragrans*), a half-hardy evergreen originally from the Far East. Minute, creamy blossoms hide in the axils of its leathery leaves where they are difficult to discern, even in daylight. Nevertheless, their presence is certain; under the still skies a refreshing perfume seeps through the darkness, cleansing the tired atmosphere of the city.

This esteemed shrub has a long history in the Orient. According to gardening author Alice Coats, the Chinese believe that the image seen in the moon is a sweet olive bush. Wu Kang, whose infidelity brought him banishment to the lunar surface, is said to continually struggle there to chop it down. The undeterred *Osmanthus* resprouts, and on clear, shining nights magically rains down seeds to earth.

Under moonlight, the sweet olive appears as a dark sentinel. Like vegetal obelisks, patriarchal specimens commonly rise to fifteen feet in height and six feet in spread. Just one of these elegant bushes suffices to fill the air with fragrance and redeem the most tedious garden terrace.

The upright habit and dense growth of the sweet olive give it a rough resemblance to privet, which is a near cousin. Like the ligustrums, it is an easy doer in most gardens, although it appreciates rich soil and shelter from strong wind. Since the tiny flowers appear on growth of the previous season, sweet olive may be clipped hard without loss of bloom; this is also an effective way to maintain these shrubs in small gardens. A trim edging of sweet olives might be planted to enclose the dark, angular parterres around a gravel-filled courtyard. This would be a fine, fragrant planting to visit in the moonlight.

Some of the hardier *Osmanthus* varieties will substitute for the cold-sensitive sweet olive in the upper South, although their potent fragrances are less pervading. A hybrid called *Osmanthus* x *fortunei* is the most worthwhile; gardeners who know it call it the tea olive. In the original form introduced from Japan in 1856, the tall shrubs produce hollylike, three-inch leaves and small, white blossoms. These are strongly scented and appear among the branches in late fall and again in spring. A twentieth-century selection from California called 'San Jose', has slightly more prickles on the foliage and offers its delicious, orange-toned blossoms in late October.

Autumn Olives

When the moon slips past the clouds to brighten the winter night even the wings of moths reflect a frothy iridescence. Most of the time these sober insects epitomize drab gray, but under the leaden glow of moonbeams their dusty, scale-coated wings seem to be formed from precious metal. Something akin to this lepidopteran skin must cover the leaves and blossoms of autumn olives (*Elaeagnus pungens*) as well, for these fragrant, gray-leafed evergreens fluoresce under similar moons.

With grayed foliage and graceful habits, the *Elaeagnus* , or silverberries, are uncommonly beautiful all year. Gardeners most appreciate them late in the fall when their honey-scented tubular flowers appear. These hang inconspicuously from lax, rambling branches and have the same gunmetal sheen and strange covering of brown and white scales as the leaves. Their fragrance is permeating, subtle, and almost always a surprise to those unfamiliar with the capacities of these plants.

The original species brought from oriental coasts, *Elaeagnus pungens*, produces a rampantly thorny, half-vining mound six-feet high. Compact selections such as 'Fruitlandii' and the spring flowering *Elaeagnus* x *ebbingei* have largely replaced it in modern gardens. These are tidy, dense bushes minus the unfriendly thorns; small crops of edible red berries come in the fall.

Variegated selections with names like 'Sunset', 'Maculata', and 'Gilt Edge' are available from some growers. These offer strikingly marked cream or gold-splashed foliage, beautiful for nocturnal planting schemes. These gilded shrubs grow weakly, however, and need to be positioned with shade and rich earth.

In contrast, one of the principal assets of the common gray *Elaeagnus* is its capacity to endure harsh conditions. These self-sufficient evergreens naturally thrive in poor, infertile soils where they develop special roots to help fix nitrogen. For casual winter-fragrant hedging, these hardy shrubs remain unsurpassed. To see their gray masses in the light of the moon and smell their honeyed autumnal perfume is to taste of the beauty of the night.

Mahonias and Jonquils

That coarse thornbushes and tender, sprouting bulbs should carry the same blossoms seems, at first, an improbable arrangement. How could two races of plants, so distinctive in form and lifestyle, agree on the same golden florets? If a gardener is at all attentive, he learns that whimsies such as this rule nature most of the time.

The clustered yellow blooms of the evergreen barberries, or mahonias, and the little golden blossoms of jonquils and narcissus seem to have been fashioned by the same artist. Both breathe sweet, honey-rich fragrances and have distinctive, cup-and-saucer shapes formed by variously ranked sepals and petals. The logic of this seems to be that these plants have chosen to attract the same winter-active pollinators, apparently bees and moths. Two very different lineages have converged on the same designs for their flowers; the consequence for gardeners is a bonanza of fragrant blossoms from winter through early spring.

Although the yellow-toned flowers of the shrubby, pinnate-leaved mahonias probably evolved to attract diurnal insects, they remain open through evening hours, dispersing fragrance on the cool, humid atmosphere. In a moonlit garden, the grapelike streamers of pallid bloom and the architectural bearing of these prickly evergreens weave a spell of enchantment.

The favorite among them is a Chinese species, the leatherleaf mahonia (*Mahonia bealei*). Initially, this seems a stiff, clumsy plant; its rigid stems, gaunt; its thorny leaves, inimical. Gardeners grow to love these curious shrubs, as any individual faithful to himself, precisely for such idiosyncrasies.

As early as December, the casually disposed primrose blooms begin dispensing fragrance from among the foliage. These waxy blossoms exhibit typical barberry construction, with outer ranks of yellowish sepals (the "saucers") around "cups" of amber petals. If not checked by undue freezes, impressive bunches of blue-dusted berries follow in spring.

In the wind-sheltered, shaded positions they enjoy, leatherleaf mahonias grow at a slow, steady pace. The clustered shoots increase from small suckers to six feet in height, where they finish in crowns of prickly, compound leaves. A branched pattern of five or more spines is embossed on each of the dull, blue-green leaflets, suggesting the thick scales of some antediluvian dragon. Nine to thirteen of these fantastic bits of greenery join together on each leaf.

The Burmese *Mahonia lomariifolia* has even more obviously reptilian ambience. Long leaves like prickly ferns appear at the tips of its vertical stems. This elegant species can be counted hardy only in the lower South, but hybrids (*Mahonia* x *media*) may be tried anywhere the leatherleaf mahonia succeeds. 'Charity', the most famous of the named forms, makes a spreading bush adorned in mid-winter by sulfury, scented blossoms held in upright candelabra.

Chinese mahonia (*Mahonia fortunei*) dispenses with the threatening prickles of these cousins. Ferny, blue-green leaves cloak its stems and partially envelop the slender clusters of pale yellow bloom that arrive in late winter. This variety is an old Chinese garden plant, hardy in most of the South, although it frequently sends out new, tender shoots in the midst of winter. In shady positions with good, leafy soil, M. *fortunei* develops a relaxed form similar to its distant cousin, nandina. Like all the Oriental mahonias, it contributes pleasant fragrances to winter evenings.

Much to be desired, also, are three distinctive mahonias of northeastern Mexico. *Mahonia gracilis* whose apt botanical name means "graceful," furnishes lax stems with wine-tinted shoots and nearly spineless, grass-green leaves. These glisten in moonlight and complement honey-scented gold blooms that erupt along the stems in February. Temperatures as low as five degrees F present no threat to these evergreens, and they seem to succeed in any soil. They look best spilling over a rocky moonlit ledge on a rugged slope.

The treelike *Mahonia chochoco* comes into full flower in December, showering fragrant yellow blossoms from branches dressed in undulate, spineless foliage. Although young plants benefit from shading, as with M. *gracilis*, this species tolerates sun, poor soil, heat, and drought unusually well for a plant of such presence. Freezes below twenty degrees F will blacken leaves and young shoots, but these sturdy fifteen-foot evergreens recover and may be counted hardy in the lower South.

In moonlight, one of the best is *Mahonia lanceolata*, whose blue-green, silver-backed foliage and open, upright habit suggest an elegant palm. The individual blossoms, large for a mahonia at one-half inch, are light yellow with darker centers. They join in amazing branched panicles to emerge from the crown of the plant in a whorl over three feet in diameter. This graceful, spineless evergreen has survived four degrees F in garden culture.

The same mild winter days that awaken such beautiful shrubs also stir their bulbous mimics, the jonquils and narcissi. These hardy representatives of the amaryllis family fashion cup-and-saucer blossoms from six outer divisions of the perianth known as "tepals" set around an inner crown, or corona. In trumpet daffodils, the corona is deep and inflated; in true narcissi it is small and shallow and sits at the end of a deep, narrow tube. It is this small-cupped section of *Narcissus* that includes most of the winter-blooming types. Like mahonias, these fragrant yellow or white flowers show handsomely in moonlight.

The bulb-flower with the strongest resemblance to the shrubby mahonias is the true jonquil (*Narcissus jonquilla*). Tiny, powerfully scented blooms the color of egg yolk appear in small clusters on its slender ten- to twelve-inch stems. Thin, rounded, dark-green leaves surround the flower stalks. At night, these miniatures look like black rushes set among streaming constellations of pale stars.

Since the waxy blossoms are less than an inch in diameter, they need to be massed if they are to have much visual presence. For fragrance, just a single bloom sprouting in a trough on the terrace suffices. Each golden floret is redolent with the scent of honey.

Several strains of *N. jonquilla* appear in gardens, differing primarily in blooming season. The best are early ones, which usually arrive in February. In the South, these naturalize in moist spots and may seed over large areas. Although not generally available from Dutch sources, true early jonquils may be collected from old gardens and are offered by a few domestic growers.

Variants like the lemony 'Baby Moon' bloom too late to be classed as winter flowers but might be added to spring gardens for their starlike blossoms. Better for night time plantings, 'Hawera' is a sulfury hybrid from a white form of *Narcissus triandrus*. It inherits a graceful nod and backswept petals, which make the tiny blossoms look like swarms of pale yellow butterflies.

Of the larger jonquils, the best winter sort is the campernelle (*Narcissus* x *odorus* 'Campernellii'), an old-fashioned flower at home in numerous yards and cemeteries. In forward seasons, blossoms show among the thick, spear-shaped leaves in February. The rich golden blooms fill the wintry atmosphere with the same powerful scent as the small jonquils. They make considerably more show with larger clusters of starry, dog-eared blossoms. Even at night these flowers paint a luminous swath over the land. Before dark masses of holly or box they glow.

Many of the wild forms of *Narcissus tazetta* attract bees with their sweet, yellow-toned blossoms, but the familiar, musk-scented paperwhites (*Narcissus tazetta* 'Papyraceus') appear to be after moths. Their parchment-white blooms and glaucous leaves seem specially designed for visibility in winter darkness, and the omnipresent, cloying fragrance could guide even blind insects in the direction of the blossoms. These cluster in loose groups on top of narrow-edged stems and appear from November into the new year. Although the flowers are often caught by freezes, these Mediterranean natives are hardy at least through the middle South. The heavy scented blossoms, so often a liability when the bulbs are potted and set indoors, have just the right potency for winter landscapes. They offer some of the most effective flowers for moonlight.

Chinese sacred lilies (*Narcissus tazetta* v. *orientalis*) are the tender cousins of paperwhites and are worth including in nocturnal plantings for their wonderfully penetrating, fruity fragrance. The sizeable blooms have broad white petals and orange cups that show nicely in the dim illumination of January moons. Fountainlike clumps of pale green leaves complement the clustered blossoms. *N. tazetta* 'Romanus', an old-fashioned sport with intensely fragrant double-petaled flowers, is also worthwhile. It appears on nursery lists as the "double Roman narcissus" or under the synonym 'Constantinople.'

With yellow disks surrounding orange cups, 'Soliel d'Or' offers radiant clusters to mix among these whites, although it is not so strong growing. As with all these tazettas, early flowering puts the bulbs at some risk from frost. They are at their best in the lower South.

Where hard freezes can be expected the starry, citron-centered Minor Monarque (*Narcissus tazetta v. italicus*) is a more reliable evening flower. Scented ivory blossoms appear in February among its deep green leaves. Even better in moonlight, 'Grand Primo' and 'Erlicheer' offer tight bouquets of pearly globes, a vision before darkly massed evergreens. 'Avalanche' provides large, yellow-eyed blossoms at the end of winter, followed closely by the yellow, amber-cupped clusters of 'Golden Dawn'. All of these sweet-scented, hardy tazettas grow happily in sun or part shade and may be planted on any soil from sand to hard clay.

The tiny hoop skirt daffodils reiterate the cups-and-saucers theme at ground level. Ribbony petals surround the impish bells of these unique midgets, which proliferate on moist, sandy soils in the southeast. The earliest are pearly forms of *Narcissus cantabricus*. 'Nylon' is particularly good, with wiry foliage and sweetly fragrant, crape-textured blooms at Christmas. Easier to obtain, *Narcissus bulbocodium v. conspicuus* is also one of the most vigorous hoop skirts. It sends up waxy golden blooms in late winter. These have no trouble catching the moonlight and will seed themselves to cover an entire hillside in time.

A novel sport offered under the name 'Golden Bells' has the capacity to explode fifteen or more one-inch blossoms from each of its marble-sized bulbs. Such tiny yellow miracles might be set to drift along a winter path and would be worth adding to pots on terraces or anywhere else their fragrant glow might challenge the winter night.

The dwarf trumpets of lent lilies (*Narcissus pseudonarcissus*) could be planted nearby to add their pale yellow and gold. These useful flowers will naturalize in most gardens but are only occasionally offered on bulb lists. The same is true for the old cream-colored variety called silver bells, with its ghostly drooping trumpets.

On sandy soils these hardy antiques may be replaced with long-cupped early cyclamineus hybrids such as 'Peeping Tom', 'February Gold', or 'Tete a

Tete'. Their short-statured golden flowers will light the way through dark winter nights and give sweet scents to fill the air when fog and gloom cover the ground.

Hyacinths and Irises

The bumbling gray moths that visit gardens in winter seem especially fond of the white French-Roman hyacinths (*Hyacinthus orientalis* v. *albulus*) that start to bloom in the bleak weeks of January. Perhaps these shiny-eyed insects are drawn by the pristine spikes of pendants bells, or they may simply follow the thick perfume that wafts on winter breezes. Such charms make these flowers enchanting in moonlight as well.

The old-fashioned white hyacinths once grew wild on the stony hills of Greece, but they have been in gardens since the first days. Their shallow growing bulbs multiply in lively patches filled with short green leaves. Blooms arrive in January and last until March, scenting the air and reflecting the moonglow like a beacon. Since they are still raised for the perfume industry and for winter forcing in pots these old bulbs are not too difficult to find on nursery lists.

Moths probably also visit the pale blue Algerian iris (*Iris unguicularis*), although the orchidlike blossoms of this family specialize mostly in pollination by bees. Tempted by nectar, the clumsy insects ordinarily crawl down between the tightly pressed upright "standards" and pendant "falls" of the iris flower, getting a good dusting of pollen in the process.

Whatever their function, the sweet blooms are such a pale shade of blue that their beauty shows even under the dim light of winter moons. When the wiry roots are settled in a suitably well-drained position, the clumps send up a succession of stems bearing the frail, beardless blossoms. In the South, these begin in November and continue intermittently through the balance of the dormant season.

Camellias and Magnolias

The silky petals of irises find shrubby analogs in the camellias blooming at the same moments. With their darkly waxed foliage the pale-flowered sorts stand out in an evening garden, though most lack a noticeable scent. To add fragrance some of the soft pink *Camellia sasanqua* varieties should be sought. 'Narigumata' is an old, lightly scented selection, with single blooms blushed a pale pink. Even more potent, hybrids are sometimes sold by nurseries under the name 'Pink Fragrance'.

These aristocratic evergreens demand rich, humusy soil and shelter from wind and strong sun. Where soils are poor or alkaline, they may be grown in prepared beds of acid peat or can be potted in tubs to offer a formal ornament year round. The pleasant, vaguely sweet blooms shatter cleanly as they fade, graciously littering the ground with their spent petals. Even in this final moment, the blossoms reflect the light of the November moons.

In the South, the early magnolias follow the camellias, so their delicate, precocious blossoms are counted as winter flowers. Of all the trees suited to gardens in moonlight, none approach the opulence of these. The plump twigs hold hundreds of fuzzy buds, which burst with the first breaths of winter warmth into blossoms like huge white or pink lilies.

The saucer magnolia (*Magnolia* x *soulangiana*) is the best known and most dependable, with large, blushed pink tulips on the ends of upright branches in January. At the same season, the star magnolia (*M. stellata*) and its more vigorous hybrid, *M.* x *loebneri*, unfold scented blooms like small, white waterlilies set among their shrubby twigs. Although the blossoms emit a thick fragrance that would seem to draw large insects, these ancient flowers came into being before creatures like moths and bees flew about the earth. This winter display is not for any of the familiar pollinators; the oversized magnolias are actually pollinated by tiny beetles.

These shrubby trees have fleshy roots that remain near the soil surface, so they are sensitive to drought and to soil compaction. Slightly raised beds dressed with generous organic mulches, partial shade, and shelter from wind are the usual keys to successful magnolia culture. In the South, these early bloomers profit from placement near shady walls or beneath the high branches of protective trees.

Small Sweets

It takes only a day or two of January warmth to awaken the sweet violets (*Viola odorata*) that carpet older gardens. In darkness, these rich purple flowers remain invisible among the densely packed, heart-shaped leaves, but if the blooms are of the fragrant sort, they may be smelled. Many modern strains have poor perfumes, but heirloom violets like the old 'Prince of Wales' are among the best-loved fragrant perennials.

Even more potent are early sweet peas (*Lathyrus odoratus*). These annual flowers come originally from southern Europe. Like other Mediterranean natives, they adapt to a winter cycle of growth in the South. Seed packets often advise spring planting, but for early flowers, the rounded peas should be pressed into the ground in October.

The old Italian strains offer the most fragrance and come in mixed shades of white, pink, lavender, or maroon held against sage green foliage.

Frostweed, *Verbesina virginica*
(Paul Cox)

Carolina jessamine, *Gelsemium sempervirens*

Winter honeysuckle,
Lonicera fragrantissima

Merril magnolia,
Magnolia x *loebneri*
'Merril' (Greg Grant)

The aggressive vines flower from January through April and usually reseed themselves in the fall. Sweet peas need a place to clamber if they are to thrive, but almost any spot that sees winter sun will do. A more delicious fate for a banal stretch of chain link could hardly be devised. In moonlight, the scented vines soften harsh elements and may be used to frame and fill empty places in the winter garden.

There is an old purple-flowered stock (*Mathiola incana*) that spicily scents the winter air in many old gardens. It has slick, dark green, oblong leaves instead of the familiar gray-dusted foliage of the double flowered strains, which come in various shades from white and cream through lavender and pink tones like the sweet peas. These easy flowers are usually listed as winter annuals but will live over a few seasons and self sow in places where they are happy.

Sweet alyssum (*Lobularia maritima*) is a cousin of the stocks (both are mustards) with honey-scented blooms that revive from summer heat to bloom through fall and winter. The white form is the favorite and the best for plantings that will be visited in the evening. These will seed themselves as a fragrant carpet if set among stepping stones or between crevices in a wall.

The same positions afford a home for the sprawling stems of the evergreen *Clematis cirrhosa*, listed in older books as *C. balearica*. The ivory petals of this species have a quiet beauty against the handsomely cut leaves. These set a shining green backdrop to the cupped blooms, which shed a light fragrance and appear intermittently through the entire winter. In spring, these ripen fluffy seed heads showier than the blossoms. Although easy in the South, this winter flower is unusual in commerce, perhaps because it becomes disheveled in late summer when it renews its foliage. This is no real failing, though, for this half creeper has much to offer in moonlight.

Daphne mezereum is a less readily kept flower, but it is worth setting out every few years for the potent incense that fills its tight fists of bloom. Although shrubby in character, daphnes belong to the mostly herbaceous spurge family and behave more like short-lived perennials than honest shrubs. They enjoy lime in the soil but resent drought and poorly aerated conditions.

By custom, these rubbery looking plants are placed in groups of three in rich, root-filled earth beneath established trees. It's a good idea to set large flat stones over the roots to keep them cool and, also, to have replacements growing in other parts of the garden for the inevitable day when these shrubs retire from the fray. For such struggles, gardeners may share precious hours with one of the most memorable of winter fragrances; without such gambles gardens would hardly be so sweet.

Viburnum farrei might be a good addition to a moonlight planting in case the daphnes fail. Little clusters of white, heliotrope-scented blossoms appear at the end of its bare twigs through the whole winter. In the lower South, *Viburnum* x *burkwoodii* is usually an early flower, too, and is equally fragrant. White forsythia (*Abeliophyllum distichum*), the golden buffalo currant (*Ribes odoratum*), and the dwarf white winter heath (*Erica* x *darleyensis* 'Silberschmelze') are others that might add pallid blooms and fragrance to winter darkness.

Spring in Winter

In the far South, there are, of course, many other winter flowers. January roses are often some of the best, and in sheltered gardens the old teas frequently drape themselves with soft petaled, fragrant blooms, ethereal under the winter moon. Where they can be counted on, pale yellows like 'Mrs Dudley Cross' and 'Souvenir du Pierre Notting' shame the best camellias and make huge glistening shrubs.

Azaleas often sputter in flower; the coppery Glen Dale hybrid 'Fashion' is especially well known for this, but there are many others. Where frost is not a continuous threat, the white calla lilies (*Zantedeschia aethiopica*) and pendant angel's trumpets (*Brugmansia* cvs.) flower through the whole of winter. Even the tender crinum lilies, especially *Crinum asiaticum* and its hybrids, add their spicy scent to the cool air.

Beauty in Moonlight

To the fragrant flowers reviewed above may be added those pale unscented blooms that help reflect the winter moonbeams. The soft yellow jasmines (*Jasminum nudiflorum*) and *J. mesnyi*, pale quinces (*Chaenomeles speciosa*), forsythias, and early-flowering peaches show an unfamiliar beauty when viewed in darkness. Evergreens and massive trees may be placed as backdrops to the many flowers of the season. In wooded gardens, the famed Lenten roses (*Helleborus foetidus*) can be left to carpet grounds with their somber chocolate blooms and gloomy foliage.

In those untended corners where frostweeds (*Verbesina virginica*) have left their crisp, dying stems, the light of the winter moon is transforming the night. As frost descends, the brown stalks that held snowy blooms for autumn butterflies are splitting under the pressure of the swelling juices within. While the sweet scents of winter flowers fade into the chill of the night, a silvery, frozen froth exudes in a delicate swirl, catching the light.

The night garden is not the place we know by day;
there seems nothing personal or familiar in its
simple masses of light and dark. We seem to have
had no hand in fashioning the vast purple gloom,
the pearly visions, the sharp, pale shapes that part
the shadows. It is not ours, nor are the tall white
forms at our side creatures grown of our fostering
love and care. Only the fragrances of the night are
familiar—Honeysuckle, White Tobacco, Stock seek
us out like the warm pressure of a hand.

LOUISE BEEBE WILDER, COLOUR IN MY GARDEN

TWO

A Moonlit Border

 lthough it is true that gardens are composed from nature and come into existence only through cooperation with natural laws, these human creations fall inherently within the province of artifice. Natural forces seek continually to return to wildness, while the tending hands of the gardener strive to maintain a sense of order, all to the favor of certain beloved flowers. The challenge is to maintain a friendly competition with nature without overwhelming her wild spirit. In this on-going struggle lies the beauty, the fascination, and the real joy of gardening.

Ideally, an overall plan for a garden provides a sort of rigid frame in which a variety of subjects can be cultivated and appreciated. Within the orderly layout, plantings may be permitted to strain against the design, overflowing on occasion in romantic abandon. In this way a thriving garden invokes many of the same charms as a tumbling ruin. One appreciates the architecture at just the moment before it is overwhelmed by nature and returned to chaos.

In the transfiguring light of the moon even strong designs can blur, so night plantings acquire a romantic sense from the start. Without colors to distract, values of light and dark come to the fore and, with bold shapes and varying textures, combine to weave a poetic tapestry in the darkness. The tender picture thus composed is often more satisfying than the same view taken in daylight. Under the serene illumination of the moon, we feel invited to inspect plants more closely, tracking mysterious scents to their floral sources as the soft plodding of our exploratory footsteps provides a heartening accompaniment.

Because most nocturnal blooms are white or yellow, gardens devoted to these flowers become somewhat monochromatic and fall within the general realm of a "white" garden. Vita Sackville-West's famous all-white garden at Sissinghurst castle has been so successful and influential that her scheme of combining silver and gray-foliaged plants with pale-colored flowers is well known among gardeners. Such silvery-gray plantings have an ethereal quality when viewed in moonlight.

By combining ordinary gray-foliaged plants, common day-blooming white flowers, and those of truly nocturnal habit, the ghostly paleness of leaves and flowers and the mysterious whirring and hovering of the night moths may be enjoyed together. Sweet, sensuous fragrances waft heavily on the night air of the moonlit garden, and the entire scheme can be directed to showcase the unique beauty of plants in cold, blue lunar light.

The rhythm of alternating shapes and textures that makes any garden beautiful shows at night in the varied plantings and in the balance of masses (plants, walls, arbors) against voids (paving, lawns, water). Invariably, the most memorable compositions evolve as a response by their owners to, as William Robinson said, "do as the ground invited them, instead of following any fixed idea as to style." Nevertheless, a comfortable, straightforward layout will not go far wrong and can show many plants at their best while making moonlight visitations especially pleasurable.

A Simple Plan

A garden planting of nocturnal blooms might begin with an entry beneath a rustic arbor. This could be inexpensively constructed with rough cedar (*Juniper*) uprights set directly into the ground. For improved night viewing, these naturally dark posts might be stripped of their fibrous bark to reveal the pale inner surface and muscular lines of the wood.

At a corner pole a rampant Himalayan musk rose such as *Rosa filipes* 'Kiftsgate' or *Rosa brunonii* 'La Mortola' could be offered a place to climb so that its luxuriant blue-green foliage and thick-scented creamy blossoms would drape as a canopy overhead. These vigorous roses are named for the famous gardens of their origin where they have smothered whole trees and even buildings. Although wickedly thorny, they make robust covers for any arbor,

River primrose, *Oenothera hookeri*

Four o'clock, *Mirabilis jalapa*

Flowering tobacco, *Nicotiana sylvestris* (Greg Grant)

Wild honeysuckle, *Gaura lindheimeri* (Greg Grant)

Jimson weed, *Datura inoxia* (Paul Cox)

and their vast, pale foliage shows nearly as well under the moon as their masses of rounded five-petaled blossoms.

After passing beneath these sensual bowers, it would be pleasing to step out onto an open court dressed in crushed gravel. This informal paving may be simply raked and spread a few inches deep wherever a hard surface is desired. Several types of gravel might be used, but crushed limestone and crushed or decomposed granite are favorites that have a pleasant appearance and offer a reassuring crunch underfoot in the darkness.

To create a double-bordered garden, this paved area of gravel might be shaped roughly like the capital letter "I", with a formal, rectangular lawn stretched down its center and linear paths along either side. Gravel terraces could fill each end of the "I", and raised borders of mixed blooms could be positioned along the sides so that the whole space of gravel and turf appears as a wide channel sunken gently into the earth. The edges of beds and lawn could be defined with simple courses of brick or stone so that the long, straight paths would be easy to follow in darkness.

The Entry Court

As visitors emerge from under the rose arbor, a view of the lawn would stretch before them. At a modest distance on the right and on the left, tall plane trees, or sycamores (*Platanus* spp.), might rise to display their patchy cream-flaked bark and pyramidal canopies of coarse, gray-felted foliage. Mexican sycamore (*Platanus mexicana*) and the southwestern strain of American sycamore (*Platanus occidentalis* var. *glabrata*) are two strong-growing and adaptable varieties, both especially silvery and worthwhile in moonlight. In summer their leafy green branches carry pale-toned young growth so that the leafy trees at night suggest deep, billowing seas capped by waves of blowing spray.

Loose arcs of dark foliage might be set to either side of these ghostly columns to enhance their effect and provide a sense of enclosure. The hybrid holly *Ilex* x 'Nellie R. Stevens' is an obliging evergreen that could be set into the gravel to create shining black curves on either side of the ter-race. If spaced a few feet apart, the upright masses of glistening, spine-tipped leaves will grow slowly to demark a punctuated ring of shrubs five- to eight-feet tall. This loose hedging creates a more potent feature in darkness than a solid wall of foliage, for the eye at night blurs detail and appreciates more open, gaunt features.

In front of these dark evergreens, contrasting mounds of silvery laven-der cotton (*Santolina chamaecyparissus*) could sprawl across the gravel to reflect the light of the moon. These invaluable plants revel in such scree plantings and in early summer will be dotted with small golden button blooms that show as brightly in the moonlight as their frothy, aromatic foliage.

An even lower ranking of dwarf juniper thymes (*Thymus rigidus* 'Peter Davis') might then be set into the gravel to offer a muddling tone of gray for this nocturnal medley. In warm climates this Sicilian native is one of the most reliable of its genus. Although not of culinary value, it makes a sturdy, ever-gray shrublet. In late spring the little branches are smothered in tiny blossoms of a lavender so pale as to approach white.

The Far Court

At the opposite end of the rectangular lawn, another gravel terrace of similar proportion would be a destination for nighttime visitations. In its middle, a small, circular pool might be set to reflect the moonbeams and reassure night-time visitors by genial splashing. Benches on either side could provide places to sit and listen to the night.

A full-moon pool might be simply constructed by burying a large galva-nized stock tank so that its lip lies just above flush with the gravel. Simple courses of brick or stone might then surround this to form a decorative edge or the silvery metal could be left exposed to catch the moonbeams. To keep waters clear, a small recirculating pump should be positioned at the bottom of the pond. This might send a stream bubbling gently onto a small artificial island so that it trickles continuously back into the pool, providing a func-tional and beautiful biological filter. A mix of stones and gravel could fill a large pot to create the islet. This, in turn, might double as support for a tall bamboo tripod that, in summer, could be entwined with the succulent stems and lavish, heart-shaped leaves of the most famous of nighttime blooms, the moon flower (*Calonyction aculeatum*).

This tropical American vine is a cousin of morning glories and will sometimes be seen listed with them as *Ipomoea alba* or *I. bona-nox*. Rather than opening its pure white, funnel-shaped blooms at dawn like its relations, the moon vine unfurls its immense long-tubed blossoms at dusk, perfuming summer evenings with the heavy clove-like fragrance of a true night bloomer. Where frost comes regularly, these tender vines are annuals, but in their native tropics they grow as rampant perennials and often lurk around lazy watercourses, draping long twining stems into the water for an extra drink. The strange green bumps and processes on the vines quickly elongate into roots when they contact water or moist earth; this aggressive grower has an insatiable appetite for food and water. It especially thrives when grown as a semi-aquatic and would make a noble summer ornament in the midst of a rounded pool dedicated to the glory of the full moon.

Behind the pond a line of tall, dark-leaved southern magnolias (*Magnolia grandiflora*) might be planted to create an enclosing, night-fragrant hedge. The lustrous laurel-like foliage of these pyramidal evergreens sometimes carries a rich brown fuzz on the undersurface called *indumentum*. This darkened medley of green and brown sets off the enormous globular flowers that unfurl from the ends of the branches on summer evenings. These opalescent bowls have an otherworldly beauty and radiate one of the most delicious of outdoor fragrances, a refreshing lemony scent like an exotic spiced tea.

Although southern magnolias become tall trees under good conditions, they shear readily, and several popular dwarf or slow-growing selections may be had. 'Little Gem', 'St. Mary's', and 'O.O. Blanchard' are three outstanding varieties ideal for a nocturnal hedgerow. If set a few feet apart and allowed to keep their branches low on the trunks, these robust cultivars will fend for themselves. An occasional light trimming or nipping of buds at the ends of the twigs will keep them in line as a hedge. For best growth, the shallow roots should be allowed an area free from competition with other plants; these magnolias might grow happily planted straight into the gravel surface at the rear of the terrace.

To augment the dark-toned foliage along the perimeter of this court, a pair of Italian stone pines (*Pinus pinea*) may be set behind the benches on either side in symmetry with the sycamores at the opposite end. These famous trees line the Appian Way near Rome, where they create a curious landscape by virtue of their mushroom shaped canopies and deep black-green needles. The reddish bark on the trunks breaks into large scales separated by wide, dark fissures, so that even in twilight the swollen stems seem like animated portions of some ancient reptile.

Italian stone pines are predisposed to soils high in lime and are fairly hardy and tolerant of drought. Young trees pass through a prolonged juvenile phase in which they maintain a thick, rounded form, but after several years the lower branches begin to shed. These fall away to reveal the characteristic shape of the adult trees; in silhouette they form fantastic dark umbrellas against the night sky.

The Lawn and Paths

Connecting these gravel courts two long, straight paths might provide access to the flower borders and frame the narrow, rectangular lawn. Since the paths would be available for walking, the import of this central turf area is not as pathway. It serves, instead, as a soft place to spread a blanket on the ground, to lay down and observe the night sky amid the flowers. With this in mind, some care should be taken in choosing a variety of grass whose surface will not collect unnecessary dew and dampness. A fine textured hybrid Zoysia like 'Emerald' or a dwarf Bermuda grass like 'tifway 419' would be good choices for keeping the ground reasonably dry at night. Lines of brick or stone might edge this lawn and separate it neatly from the gravel pathways.

The Raised Borders

The greater quantity of flowers would reside in the double raised beds on either side of the two long paths. Raising the soil in these borders provides a simple landscape device to put the plants on stage and improve the visual structure of the planting. This rise need not be unnecessarily grand but should be enough to be perceived even in the pale light of the moon.

A short ledge of stones or stacked brick near the edges of the paths might retain a small vertical displacement of eight or ten inches, with beds sloping gradually upwards from this point. At ten feet back the borders might reach a maximum height of three feet above grade. With sides gently inclined in this fashion, the central terrace takes on a configuration reminiscent of the ancient ball courts of Central America, where hard rubber globes bounced off the tilted slopes during ceremonial games.

To give the nocturnal borders definition and provide a backdrop for the mixed collections of pale flowers and foliage that will fill them, lines of tall, dark-foliaged conifers might be planted as an enclosure. Rapid growers like the formally upright *Juniperus chinensis* 'Ketleerii' would be excellent for such screening, noble in moonlight when the crops of steel blue berries shine against the dark foliage. Rows of the rustic *Juniperus virginiana* 'Canaertii' would be even better, maturing to a half wild tangle of dark, thrusting branches, boldly stabbing into the night sky. This old juniper is not as popular as it once was but is still worth planting for its distinctive form, like a loosely stacked pyramid of fat green arms, eventually fifteen- to twenty-feet tall. In winter 'Canaertii' also carries sprays of small blue berries, though these are not as large and showy as the ones on 'Ketleerii'.

To catch the evening breezes and add their gentle rustlings to the night, several clumps of variegated giant cane (*Arundo donax* 'Variegata') might be set before this backdrop of conifers. This half woody grass is deciduous in cold weather but resprouts in spring with masses of creamy striped foliage like lush stalks of corn. The bold variegation fades as the season progresses but offers a torch of pale color in spring and early summer.

Other pale-leaved grasses like the ivory striped *Miscanthus sinensis* 'Cabaret' or the silvery blue lyme grass (*Elymus arenarius* 'Findhorn') would also be fine in moonlight. The first makes a tall clump of arched creamy blades, the second suckers and spreads in patches of stiff, upright blue, striking as a mid-row subject.

The white seed heads of the silver fountain grass (*Pennisetum villosum*) would be elegant in moonlight, and this rugged variety should certainly be included in the plantings. Although not especially pale, the featherlike seeds of the wiregrass (*Stipa tenuissima*) have a satiny sheen that captures moonbeams in a unique fashion, reflecting an eerie glow over plantings. This cool-season grower makes short, arching clumps of slender evergreen foliage and serves well as an accent or ground cover, thriving especially in the dry soil at the base of trees.

Where there is room in the borders, a few distinctive specimen trees might be positioned along with the grasses. It would be difficult to imagine anything more effective at night than several white-flowered crape myrtles, with their patchy, exfoliating bark and lithe, bone-colored trunks. Needing minimal attention beyond occasional thinning of the branches and a steady supply of moisture in summer, these Oriental trees improve in grace when left to grow naturally as multi-stemmed trees. Their tremendously long blooming season brings universal admiration; in the South it usually lasts the whole of summer.

'Glendora White' is an old selection of common crape myrtle (*Lagerstroemia indica*) with especially lustrous, rounded leaves and large trusses of clear white, honey-scented blossoms. This variant is one of the most reliable "indica" types, maturing at a useful eight to ten feet. It might be planted in formal lines of three or five trees on either side of the raised borders.

Even more notable for its peeling, multicolored bark, an uncommon Japanese crape myrtle, *Lagerstroemia fauriei* offers spectral beauty with light-green, lacy foliage, vase-shaped growth, and triangular masses of small white blooms. The original trees of this ghostly species were discovered by John Creech in 1957 growing in a mountain forest above Kurio on the island of Yakushima. 'Natchez', a robust hybrid, is easier to find in nurseries than *L. fauriei* itself. It offers mottled cinnamon and ivory bark, willowy stems, and white flowers. These crape myrtles commonly reach fifteen to twenty feet at maturity.

White flowers such as these show starkly in moonlight, but they are not the only possibilities for a nocturnal planting, because any pale blossom, whatever its shade, can be utilized. For instance, the light-pink indica crape myrtle 'Near East', with its long, semi-pendant panicles, would be as decorative in moonlight as any of the white-flowered types. With this in mind, the moonlit border can be allowed to depart somewhat from the ordinary constraints of the monochromatic "white garden," though this has its charms.

Several flowering shrubs may be sought to add year-round structure for the plantings, and here the old white-flowered Persian musk rose 'Nastarana' would be especially fine, with clusters of thick-scented blooms through the growing season. This is a dwarf cousin of the vining musk roses on the arbor and makes an everblooming bush three feet tall and wide.

The fragrant white butterfly bush (*Buddleia asiatica*) might be another good shrub for the nocturnal displays, with arching stems and pointed clusters of tiny blooms. White selections of the common butterfly bush (*Buddleia davidii*) would be valuable for their gray-toned foliage, even though they lack evening fragrance.

Sweet-scented mock oranges (*Philadelphus* ssp.) turn to clouds of snow in late spring, and space ought to be found for at least one of these old-fashioned treasures. 'Natchez,' a single-flowered introduction discovered in an old garden in Natchez, Mississippi, is particularly elegant. This selection needs a couple of years to establish before blooming heavily.

Although there are tender jasmines with better night fragrances, the hardy Florida jasmine (*Jasminum floridum*) bears numerous clusters of small yellow blooms over a long season and would be worth including in the borders. The flowers show splendidly against the arching evergreen foliage, glowing in the light of the moon like hundreds of tiny stars. The tiny white trumpets of the Chinese abelia (*Abelia chinensis*) would also be pleasant to add for summer display. This old form is more fragrant than the common abelia hybrids. The hardy plants are rugged and handsome, with lacy evergreen foliage. Other good shrubs include white flowered single althaea or rose-of-Sharon (*Hibiscus syriacus*) and the gold-bossed St. John's wort (*Hypericum calycinum*).

A Few Night Flowers

With the beds defined and these woody plants in place, a varied array of annual and perennial flowers can be encouraged to sprawl through the beds. These lusty growers really offer much of the fun in gardening and are the surest route to quick, successful effects.

The most commonly lauded of the nocturnal bedding flowers, the ornamental tobaccos (*Nicotiana*) are the flowering cousins of the true smoking tobacco from South America. Originally, this genus of tender perennials became popular for a creamy white, sweet-scented species, *Nicotiana alata*. Its drooping blooms typify the routine pursued by many night-blooming plants.

The tubular blossoms attract certain long-tongued hawkmoths of the family *Sphingidae*, popularly known as *Sphinx* moths. At rest, the torpedo-shaped bodies of these moths hold their striped or patterned wings raked back at a characteristic 45-degree angle, but it is more common to see the odd creatures hovering over evening flowers, wings lost in a blur of furious whirring. *Sphinx* moths sip nectar using lengthy tongues to reach down as they hang in the air like hummingbirds. Just how long these organs are becomes apparent when one of the underground pupae is discovered, for at this stage the brownish insects retain the proboscis in a peculiar handle or "tongue case" beneath the head.

Not only do hawkmoths visit tobaccos for nectar, but some species also come to feed upon the plants. The larvae of one especially large and common species, *Manduca sexta*, is the famous tobacco hornworm, a common pest of *Nicotiana* and related members of the nightshade family (*Solanaceae*) like tomatoes. Here the association between plant and insect is complete. Although sometimes a victim of the caterpillar's appetite, *Nicotiana* depends on the adult moths for pollination and actually closes its blooms during daylight hours. It is only late in the afternoon and at night when the favored hawkmoths are active that the greenish blossoms expand to reveal the chalky interiors of their little five-petaled stars and send out their thick, jasminelike fragrance.

This charming natural history lesson might fill a moonlit border with wonder, but first one must actually manage to find seeds of these old bedding flowers. To many a gardener's consternation, it is now easy to obtain the colorful but scentless horticultural strains of flowering tobacco (*Nicotiana* x *sanderae*), but it usually demands a determined effort to search out and acquire the old-fashioned fragrant form of the species.

In fact it is often easier to locate a rare white-flowered cousin from Argentina, *Nicotiana sylvestris*. This is an elegantly tall, fragrant bloom in itself and is worth planting for its lyre-shaped rich green foliage and pendant clusters of twenty or more nocturnal trumpets, even if the true *N. alata* can be had. In the South, *N. sylvestris* will often live over for several seasons where conditions are to its liking.

Although the ordinary annual strains of "flowering tobacco" offered in the trade lack real fragrance, they do provide some wonderfully pale colors for moonlit plantings. Glowing green, mushroom white, dull olive tinged with rose, or delicate apricot may be had among the modern mixes of *Nicotiana*, as well as the more usual dark reds, bright pinks, and rich maroons. In mixed plantings the subtle gradation of the various shades produces an enchanting effect.

The same can be said for the old strains of the petunia, another member of the nightshade family from South America. Our garden hybrids derive from two wild species, a purple day bloomer from Argentina (*Petunia violacea*) and a fragrant night-flowering variety from Brazil with large chalky blossoms (*P. axillaris*). The soft, sweet fragrance of this wild species carries on into many, though not all, of the modern petunia hybrids, which now have been bred in superb variety.

Wonderful though these domesticates may be for daytime bedding displays, the most bewitching effects under moonlight usually appear among garden mongrels lurking in old neglected yards, vacant lots, and waste places. The flowers of these naturalized types come haphazardly in mixed lavenders, whites, and various pale shades from purple to mauve. Gratefully, breeders have begun to pay attention to the charms of the old varicolored petunias and are now busy reintroducing similar strains with the sweet fragrance and soft, clear colors of the "multifloras." These would be good flowers for the front of night borders where their trailing stems could sprawl over paths and their floppy blossoms could be lifted for a whiff of evening fragrance.

Of course the jimson weed (Datura inoxia) would have a prominent place in the night border for its oversized, jasmine-scented funnels. This southwestern flower is known to many nongardeners from its portrait in a famous Georgia O'Keefe painting. The painting captures the mysterious ambiance of the snowy blooms, with their curling petal tips and creased and folded trumpets. The huge upfacing blossoms appear among coarse, felted leaves on summer evenings, flagging the following morning as they darken to purplish tones. Later, prickly fruits ("thorn apples") hang down from the stems and ripen seeds to volunteer on rough, open ground. Of the many flowers in this genus, D. inoxia is the most generally adapted, showing a decided preference for poor, dry soils where its carrotlike perennial root can grow deeply. It thrives in almost any garden where it is offered bright sun and good drainage.

Some of the handsome fruiting members of the nightshade family might be included among the flowers, for there is no reason to consign such attractive plants to the vegetable patch when they might beautify ornamental gardens. The yellow pear tomato is a hardy heirloom variety with cherry-sized amber berries that show happily under moonbeams. The lavish foliage of these indeterminate vines also feeds larvae of the five-spotted hawkmoth, or tomato hornworm (Manduca quinquemaculata), which visits these and other night flowers.

Even prettier in moonlight, yellow or white forms of eggplants might make tidy bushes of an abundantly fruitful presence. 'White Beauty' is a popular strain whose small lavender blooms ripen over many weeks of summer to large white globes. These peer out among from among the coarse, wavy foliage, making a handsome picture in the gloom. 'Asian Bride' and 'Rosa Bianca' are other pale-fruited sorts offered by seed specialists.

The remarkable river primrose (Oenothera hookeri) is one of the indispensable flowers for night borders; its three-inch clear yellow blooms literally open before gardener's eyes. This event occurs a few hours after nightfall, but before midnight, and seems like a slow motion film. The four-petaled blossoms, united into twisted golden funnels, swell until they reach a point of release, unfurling suddenly to lemony open chalices. This abrupt expansion turns darkness into light and makes the active flowers at the tips of the branches seem like the hungry polyps of some gigantic coral.

This large-growing species usually behaves as a biennial and spends its first season making leafy rosettes. The following summer these bolt into woody bushes three- to four-feet tall, covered from midsummer onwards with masses of clear yellow, lightly fragrant blooms. O. hookeri is a native of gravely stream banks in the West and Midwest and seems to thrive everywhere in gardens. In the North, a somewhat smaller cousin, Oenothera erythrosepala, offers similar but slightly less dramatic effects.

A better behaved perennial, the fluttermill (Oenothera macrocarpa) has been known to gardeners for years as Missouri primrose or Oenothera missouriensis. These tough plants hail from limestone soils of the Ozark plateau and the southern Great Plains, where they root deeply in the shallow, rocky ground. Sprawling stems, covered in tapered waxy foliage, carry the long-tubed yellow blooms through summer. Papery four-winged seed pods ripen in autumn, earning for these plants the quaint name "fluttermill."

This is a first-class flower for fronts of borders, where the custard-scented, lemony blooms can be enjoyed from dusk through the following day. Although usually endowed with green foliage, a race from the high plains, variety incana, has silvery leaves that make it an even better accompaniment in moonlight. All forms are hardy, heat and drought tolerant. They are easy to grow in any well-drained, sunny position.

Another member of the evening primrose family (Onagraceae), Lindheimer's butterflies (Gaura lindheimeri) might be added to the night borders for its airy clouds of cream-colored blossoms. These seem to be magically suspended above the body of the plant on a gossamer frame of thin, wiry stems. With four milky, upturned petals centered over bosses of purple-red stamens, the little blooms exude an orchidlike beauty. They charm all who see them, blushing pink as they fade.

The heat-loving plants are long blooming and add a sprightly note to summer beds in spite of their demure coloring. They have become universal favorites in American gardens. Slightly woody stems support the flower stalks and carry the modest clusters of leathery leaves through the summer. These die down to purplish, overwintering rosettes each fall.

Gaura lindheimeri is a native of rough prairies in southeast Texas and Louisiana, a preparation that seems to have adapted it for garden life everywhere. For collectors there is a form with variegated leaves (although this is not strong growing in hot sun) and a light pink cultivar, 'Siskiyou Pink' (although this would be of limited value in moonlight).

Moonvine,
Calonyction aculeatum
(Greg Grant)

Silver-leaf fluttermill, *Oenothera macrocarpa* v.
incana (Paul Cox)

Persian musk rose, *Rosa* cv. 'Nastarana'
with *Ballota pseudodictamnus*

Bells of Ireland, *Moluccella laevis*

Spider flower, *Cleome hasslerana*

Spider flowers (*Cleome hasslerana*) might be set nearby in the middle ranks of the borders for their upright, leafy stems and crowns of loose white or lavender-pink pompoms. These peculiar night flowers have long trailing stamens that project from the butterflied blossoms like little bomb bursts. This must be very attractive to the summer moths, for they swarm over these feathery blooms every evening.

Cleome is a tropical American representative of the caperbush family (*Capparaceae*) and displays the amazing tolerance to heat and poor soil typical of its clan. The delicate, spidery blooms manage a graceful appearance even in wilting temperatures and show vividly under the pale light of the moon. Like the old petunias, these rugged plants have a welcome habit of returning from self-sown seed.

The yellow-flowered forms of four o'clock, or wonder of Peru (*Mirabilis jalapa*), are equally forgiving and suitable for the night borders. Although fast enough when planted from seed to be listed among annuals, in the South these old favorites might more naturally fall among the perennials, for the plants produce a tough, turniplike root that endows them with great drought tolerance and nearly guarantees their return the following spring. Four o'clocks often persist in abandoned yards without any care whatsoever and prove ideal for tough positions in dry soil and partial shade.

True to name, these blossoms open late each afternoon, remaining fresh through the evening hours and into the following morning. The yellowish forms have more fragrance than the red, rose, and purplish strains and are the most rewarding for night plantings. Their two-inch, trumpet-shaped flowers usually ripen seed that comes reasonably true to color, so yellows can be selected by roguing out unwanted forms from plantings of mixed shades, which is the way four o'clocks are usually sold.

Several perennial members of the pink family (*Caryophyllaceae*) carry pronounced night scents, but most keep their flowers open through daytime so that few outward clues can be found to their nocturnal affinities. One common and dependable sort is the old-fashioned bouncing bet, or soapwort (*Saponaria officinalis*). In the sun, the washy mauve-pink blooms of this antique border flower seem to sag above its matted green foliage. At twilight the delicately tinted blossoms revive and freshen, and as night falls they lift and send forth a sweet perfume. This is irresistible to the hoards of moths making their evening forays.

The double pink form of the species, 'Roseo Plena', is the best one to choose for garden planting, for it is sterile and puts its energy into making flowers rather than seed. This is a very old garden perennial, useful as a foreground plant in part sun, or in shade in the South. It would be nice spilling over rocks at the front of the border and is rugged and leafy enough to recommend as a ground cover.

Several *Dianthus* with extraordinarily lacy deep-cut petals are also night fragrant. The most popular of these floral snowflakes is an oriental species, *Dianthus superbus*. These hardy flowers are more accepting of heat and humidity than most dianthus and make tidy tufts of slender green foliage. They will self sow where conditions are to their liking, in the South these are the most reliable night blooming members of the pink family. 'Cupid's Lace' and 'Loveliness' are two seed strains with long blooming seasons and a range of colors from white to deep rose.

Night stock (*Mathiola longipetala*) and sweet rocket (*Hesperis matronalis*) are two famous night-fragrant members of the mustard family (*Cruciferae*) that might be added to the borders seasonally. The first is a drab brownish-purple annual; the second, whose Latin name (*Hesperis*) recalls the evening star, is a biennial that should be reseeded each year to keep its white and purple blooms coming along. Like true stocks, these Old World natives thrive best in climates with long cool periods but may be cultivated in the South if seeded in late autumn. The rugged plants thrive on gritty or rubbly soils and might be set into crevices between stones along the edge of the borders. Their four-petaled blossoms arrive in spring and expand with sweet, spicy scents that are most potent at night.

Other favorite cool-weather plants that might be added to the moonlight display include green-towered bells-of-Ireland (*Moluccella laevis*), feathery white lace flower (*Ammi majus*), light bluish throatwort (*Trachelium caeruleum*), and pale, globular, blue lace flower (*Trachymene coerulea*). The first three are Mediterranean natives, hardy in the South when sown in the fall for spring bloom. The last hails from Australia and will want to be started indoors and set out after the last frost of spring if its beautiful, long-tubed blossoms, like a pale lavender Queen Anne's Lace, are to perfect themselves before the onset of summer heat.

Decorative Foliage

Plants with gray foliage can provide a strong counterpoint for these night flowers and are interesting even when not in bloom. The silver leaf sunflower (*Helianthus argophyllus*) is one that would be especially arresting in moonlight. Its vast castles of gray-felted leaves perch with flocks of large yellow, chocolate-centered sun blossoms all summer. The monstrous annuals may reach six feet by the end of the growing season.

A native of sand dunes along the gulf of Mexico, this easy-growing wildflower has been overlooked for many years. With increased interest in sunflowers as cut blossoms, H. *argophyllus* is making its way into gardens where destiny is sure to bring it under the glowing beams of the moon. Its hoary masses of foliage fluoresce from the moment the seeds sprout and the coarse leaves begin building their silvery towers.

The ever popular dusty millers (*Senecio cineraria*) certainly deserve consideration for their silvery shrublets, dotted on occasion with small yellow daisies. 'White Diamond' is a select form with felted paddle-shaped leaves that show better in darkness than the ordinary cut-leaved strains. These are hardy in the South.

Another similar silvery plant that sometimes shares the common name of "dusty miller," *Centaurea cineraria* makes an ever-gray mound of gracefully scalloped foliage, ethereal in the gloom of night. The pale blooms, like lavender cornflowers, appear sparingly if at all. This grows as a perennial in the lower South and makes a useful bedding plant elsewhere.

The filigreed artemisias are probably the best loved of the little gray bushes and include numerous varieties for flower gardens. A hybrid between the common European wormwood (*Artemisia absinthium*) and the tree artemisia of the Mediterranean (*A. arborescens*), called 'Powis Castle', is invaluable where its steely gray masses can be allowed to sprawl. Unlike other artemisias, this versatile plant is sterile, so its displays of frothy gray are never marred by the inconsequential blooms common to this genus.

The spreading evergreen mats of the fernlike yarrows would be delightful for the front of the borders, especially the silver-leafed hybrid *Achillea* 'Moonshine', aptly named for its creamy yellow blossoms. Its flattened, plate-like flowers appear on twelve- to eighteen-inch stems throughout summer, visibly glowing in the barest illumination. The hardy plants derive from *Achillea clypeolata* and *A. taygetea*, two natives of the Mediterranean basin, so 'Moonshine' inherits excellent tolerance to poor soil and drought.

Any of the many *Dianthus* with gray, tufted foliage might be set along the front of the plantings with these to catch the moonbeams. The dwarf border carnations are especially fine, and their silver-toned mounds provide a continuing treat, even when the clove-scented blooms have finished.

Also enchanting, but seldom employed outside of herb beds, the dwarf or salad burnet (*Sanguisorba minor*) provides gray-tufted fernlike clumps for edgings. These are especially charming when dew collects along the serrations on the edges of the leaves, as it does most evenings. The little drops capture the moonglow, lighting up like tiny crystal balls. As a bonus, the foliage is edible, with a flavor and aroma like fresh cucumbers. The lush plants are surprisingly tough and resistant to drought, for they hail from the stony hillsides of Greece.

Some larger notes of gray might be created by clumps of artichokes or cardoons, which also come from the Mediterranean. These massive cousins of the thistles enjoy rich soils and plenty of moisture. When well treated, they produce fountains of gray, ruffled leaves rivaled by few other plants. In the South they perform best in positions shaded from hot sun.

Although homely and forlorn in daylight, at night the bold upthrusting spikes and dewy rosettes of common mullein (*Verbascum thapsus*) seem noble. Originally native in southern Europe, this robust biennial is now widely naturalized in North America. It makes itself at home in any garden where it gets sun and good drainage. The soft yellow, tubular blossoms embed in a hairy four-foot spike that rises from the ragged leaves at the end of the plant's second season. The nocturnal flowers open a few at a time on summer evenings, marking the culmination of the mullein's career. While intriguingly tall in bloom, the real value of the plants is in the beauty of their first-year rosettes, which catch the moonbeams as well as any foliage.

The huge leaves of the silver sage (*Salvia argentea*) amaze with covers of velvet whiteness as cold as lunar light. Like the mulleins they make biennial rosettes; the white flowers come during the second season.

Likewise, plush lamb's ears (*Stachys byzantina*) makes a silver mass of soft felted leaves invaluable for the verges of the night border. This touchable plant is too well known to warrant description, but its cultural requirements, full sun and perfect drainage, are worth repeating. In the South the prostrate mounds benefit from division each fall—this keeps stems from becoming crowded and rotting at the center as sometimes happens during warm, humid periods. 'Silver Carpet' is a nonblooming selection that seems less susceptible to this calamity.

The classic gray foliage of the lavenders (*Lavandula* spp.) also has trouble in warm climates, so if these are to play a part in the night displays, some care should be given to selection. The gray form of the French lavender (*Lavandula dentata*) is one that is good in warmer areas, but it must be protected from any hard frost. A recent hybrid, 'Goodwin Creek', seems to combine tolerance of cold, warmth, and humidity with nice silver leaves and rich blue flowers, although like all lavenders, it demands good drainage. The airy sprays of the Russian sage (*Perovskia atriplicifolia*) offer many of the same charms of grayed foliage and light-toned bloom seen in the lavenders and are a good deal easier to grow.

A large-flowered rose mallow native to the southeastern states, *Hibiscus grandiflorus*, should be mentioned for its floppy white blooms and felted maplelike foliage. These ruggedly coarse leaves reflect moonbeams with ease and appear on hardy, easy-growing perennials that reach four to five feet in height. The rugged plants return each summer from tough, carrotlike rootstocks; few subjects are so striking in moonlight.

Another majestic source of blue-gray, the African bee balm (*Melianthus major)* becomes a small-mounded shrub to four feet. Although short-lived in the South, these exotic soft-wooded plants grow quickly and project a unique beauty with their compound foliage, curved and feathered into a serrated mass of silver. Curious but inconspicuous flowers hang beneath the leaves in spring and fill with a sweet black nectar. The lesser bee-brush, *Melianthus minor,* has more fine-textured foliage and honey-scented flowers of similar value.

To make these silvery plants count, the night borders may employ a few good dark leaves as well. Purplish cannas like the old *Canna warscewiczii* would offer a bold contrast to the pale foliage and flowers, rising as dark masses four- to six-feet tall. Although deep toned, the succulent leaves of these plants are translucent, and in a strange muted way they will actually transmit the pale light of the moon.

To sprawl along the foreground of the beds, the invaluable purple heart (*Setcreasea pallida*) might be set to offer its purple leaves and lilac-pink blossoms. In the middle rows, dark-leaved selections of shrubs like purple smoke-tree (*Cotinus coggygria* 'Royal Purple'), dwarf purple peach (*Prunus peusica*), Chinese fringeflower (*Loropetalum chinense* 'Plum Delight'), or Japanese barberry (*Berberis Thunbergii* 'Rose Glow') could add masses of blackness to meld with the light-colored leaves and flowers elsewhere in the borders.

To finish the medley of foliage and blossom in these borders the whole array of pale blooms will need to be explored, from early spring bulbs like snowflakes (*Leucojum aestivum*) to the massive crinums and tall regal lilies (*Lilium regale*) of summer. The torchlike spikes of white summer phloxes (*Phlox paniculata* 'Mt. Fuji'), night-fragrant daylilies like the old yellow *Hemerocallis* 'Hyperion', the tall spires of pale yellow hollyhocks (*Alcea rugosa*), the drooping petals of white coneflowers (*Echinacea purpurea* 'White Swan'), and the massive ivory trusses of Spanish bayonets (*Yucca gloriosa*) will all find ways into the night borders. Pearly fruits of white beautyberries (*Callicarpa americana* 'Laetea') and cascading snowberries (*Symphoricarpos albus*) will be found to carry the composition even into autumn and winter. As the light of the moon plays over the wondrous array the night border will have become a magnificent universe unto itself.

The sleep of plants must be a very light one, and
stirred by many ambitious dreams.

WILLIAM BEEBE, NONSUCH

THREE

The Forest Moon

 uch of the quiet activity of the plant kingdom proceeds through the night, for under the distant glow of moon and stars lengthening stems and expanding leaves, plants accomplish their principal task: continued growth. Tramping through a darkened woodland often brings a sense of this process. At night the leafy groves nearly always smell of the vigor of their inhabitants. Like the cleansing breath of some nocturnal sylvan spirit, a cool freshness pervades the air of the living forest and speaks of the abundance and supremacy of this verdant architecture.

Gardeners fortunate enough to have a woodland to plant can share evenings with a variety of shade-loving flowers and shrubs suited to the leafy, root-filled soils of the forest understory. Many are ideal candidates for the moonlit garden, possessed of the requisite features of pallid bloom and sweet, penetrating fragrance. With scorching sunlight tempered by overhanging branches, delicate cream- and ivory-splashed leaves of variegated plants can be positioned to make the most of darkened places under the woodland canopy. Simple foliage compositions of varied tones of lightness, darkness, and reflectivity will make visual poems of the dappled shade beneath the trees, serene in the day as well as in the diffuse lighting of the moon.

The most desirable canopies come from lacy-leafed trees with deep root systems, for these offer gently filtered light yet leave ample moisture in the soil for underplantings. In the South the slender-needled longleaf and loblolly pines offer accommodating environments of this sort. Slightly denser shade cast by mixed hardwoods such as oaks, hickories, or maples can be good for plants that enjoy the deep layers of leaf litter that accumulate beneath such cover. Forest soils will generally be drier and thinner under alkaline conditions, but native woodlands of oak, cedar elm, or pecan in the Southwest can provide habitats for a variety of shade-loving subjects.

New gardens without established tree cover will need to develop an overstory before a woodland garden can be planted. Yet, even on treeless lots, a few shady, moist areas may be found near north foundations of the house or walls. By planting trees adjacent to these places, a wooded area can be extended and developed in just a few seasons. Pines, oaks, pecans, maples, and deeply rooted elms like cedar elm (*Ulmus crassifolia*) offer the best cover for future gardens. Aggressively fast shade trees such as ash, mulberry, or sycamore should usually be avoided, because their shallow roots compete for moisture.

Trees in Moonlight

Several decorative trees might be highlighted within the forest to enhance the beauty of the woodland. Where there is room for a large oak, the chinquapin (*Quercus muehlenbergii*) could be worthwhile. Its serrated silver-backed leaves and flaky, grayed bark reveal a gentle sympathy with the cold tones of the moonbeams. At night these tall oaks erupt through the forest like pale-toned geysers. The drought-resistant chinquapins grow rapidly on shallow rocky or alkaline soils and make excellent garden trees. Other adaptable hardwoods with interesting glaucous-backed foliage include chalk maple (*Acer* x *leucoderme*) and Mexican maple (*Acer skutchii*).

In the rich cypress woods surrounding the city of Mobile, Alabama, breezes off the Gulf continually stir the forest to masses of silver, for the damp, acid lowlands fill with the lush greenery of sweet bays (*Magnolia virginiana*). The large pale green leaves of these native magnolias are coated beneath with a luminous white powder, so that when the oblong foliage blows in the wind its glaucous underside flashes through the forest like flocks of white birds.

In contrast to other magnolias, this is an easy tree to grow on damp and even soggy soils, although it is prone to mineral deficiencies on dry alkaline ground. The creamy white flowers smell deliciously of oranges mixed with attar of roses and open from tight velvety buds held at the ends of the stems in early summer. Although the globular blooms open late in the afternoon and close partially at night, opening fully and finally on their second morning, their penetrating aroma is an evening feature and the whole rubbery presence of these primitive plants has much to offer in moonlight.

There are several horticultural variations in sweet bay; its native range extends from Texas to Massachusetts. Northern forms tend to be shrubby and deciduous. Along the central Gulf, these magnolias are usually evergreen and treelike. This larger southern form is sometimes referred to as variety *australis* and has long-lasting, lemon-scented flowers. Texas strains resemble *australis* in size and fragrance but are markedly deciduous. In some especially fine forms of sweet bay, the creamy blossoms exhibit a greenish glow at the

Liriope spicata 'Silver dragon' surrounding
Heuchera micrantha 'Palace Purple'

A darkened wood

Shelf fungi growing on deadfall

Hoary azalea, *Rhododendron canescens*

base of the petals. For collectors there is a unique dwarf with miniaturized leaves and foliage.

Several other magnolias make worthwhile subjects for woodland plantings under the moon. In gardens sheltered from wind, few plants could rival the big-leaf magnolia (*Magnolia macrophylla*) with its dramatic yard-long, white-backed leaves and enormous pink-zoned blossoms. This native tree is a denizen of rich woodlands and needs superlative conditions (moist, acid soil and ideal drainage) to perfect its development. M. *ashei* is a rare shrub-sized variant with similar cultural needs. A vigorous Mexican cousin (M. *dealbata*) could probably accept less optimum soils and exposures, though it too is a tree of deep, primeval forests. Summer-flowering Asian species like the evergreen *Magnolia delavyi* and the silver-barked *Magnolia hypoleuca* are other varieties worth having where soils are well developed; these exotic species are hardy in the middle and lower South, offering especially handsome silver and green foliage and creamy blossoms that show up well at night.

During the 1970s plant breeders associated with the Brooklyn Botanic Gardens developed an intriguing yellow-toned magnolia called 'Elizabeth' from a cross of the cucumber leafed magnolia of the eastern states (*Magnolia acuminata*) and the white-blossomed oriental yulan magnolia (*Magnolia heptapeta*). 'Elizabeth' is an easy garden plant for the middle and upper South, with pleasantly fragrant, clear yellow blossoms in late spring. This hybrid would be a fine tree to encounter in the pale illumination of an April moon.

Later in the spring the chartreuse blooms of a magnolia cousin, the tulip poplar (*Liriodendron tulipifera*) might add their ethereal beauty to the night, as well. With unique lobed foliage, these odd, prehistoric-looking trees offer a striking texture even when they are not in bloom. Tulip poplars can become surprisingly large on good moist soil.

Under more general conditions in the South and Southwest, the varied forms of southern magnolia (M. *grandiflora*) provide waxy-leafed evergreens suited to more sun, drought, and alkalinity than their finicky cousins. At night selections of this adaptable species create towers of glistening foliage lit also by massive, fragrant blossoms. Since fleshy roots ramble near the soil surface, these are not easy trees to garden under but are worth including in woodland plantings, especially where other magnolias cannot be represented. Named forms as well as seedling trees may be had from nurseries; a hybrid of southern magnolia with sweet bay, *Magnolia* x *freemani* 'Timeless Beauty', is worth planting for its outstanding fragrance.

Just as these glossy broad-leafed trees reflect the moonlight, many needle-leaved conifers will shine at night, though they are dark, flowerless, and somber in the day. Varieties that can be positioned in the understory of the forest are especially good. Chinese yew (*Taxus chinensis*), Chinese plum yew (*Cephalotaxus fortunei*), Florida torreya (*Torreya taxifolia*), and China-fir (*Cunninghamia fortunei*) are lacy-leaved evergreens adapted to shady gardens in the South. On moon-filled nights their darkened tents of sharp pointed leaves sparkle with borrowed brightness.

The Value of Gold

In autumn any of the forest trees whose leaves turn towards yellow make a show in the moonlight, so several might be added to plantings for their nocturnal effects. Selections of green ash (*Fraxinus pennsylvanica* v. *lanceolata*) like 'Summit' or 'Marshall' and variants of sugar maple like Caddo maple (*Acer saccharum* 'Caddo') seem especially suitable for their rich autumn coloring.

Even more renowned, the maidenhair tree (*Ginkgo biloba*) is a living relict of antediluvian forests, unchanged from the days when pterodactyls darted among its branches. The oddly triangular pale green leaves, veined fan-wise like fronds of the maidenhair fern, turn to buttery tones over several weeks of the fall. As these leathery leaflets cascade from the tall spreading branches, they light the autumn garden like no other foliage. A night encounter with these fallen shreds of gold littering the earth along a dim forest path confirms the mystic nature of these trees, which have been nurtured and preserved in sacred groves of the Orient over the centuries. Although slow growing in the South, ginkgos are long lived and pest free and accept a wide range of conditions.

Many of the small flowering trees of spring also give good yellow tones that might be dispersed under the canopy of taller trees. Redbuds (*Cercis canadensis*) are middle layer subjects that prove to be reliable sources of autumnal gold and may be had in excellent white-flowered selections such as 'Alba' and 'White Texas' suitable for moonlight displays. Delicate traceries of pea blossoms line their gray stems at the beginning of spring and magically light up the darkest woodland. These white redbuds reach ten feet or so in height and make fine trees to plant where they receive shading at least half of the day.

Buckeyes (*Aesculus* spp.) also turn mostly to yellow tones in autumn. Under moonlight the lemon-tinted yellow buckeye (*Aesculus pavia* v. *flavescens*), cream-colored Texas buckeye (*A. arguta*), and white bottlebrush buckeye (*A. parviflora*) would be worthwhile understory subjects, maturing to small trees eight- to ten-feet tall. Their coarse palmate foliage requires thorough shading if it is to hold through summer, but these thick-stemmed spring flowering trees are otherwise rugged and adaptable. A distant cousin native to rocky hills in the Southwest, the pink-flowered Mexican buckeye (*Ungnadia speciosa*) is another superb source of autumn yellow.

Spring Whites

White-flowered trees of all sorts are good in moonlight, so these can be added to the forest for their luminous, fragrant value. One of the most imposing is yellowwood (*Cladrastis kentukea*), a native of southern mountains with coarse pinnate leaves and drooping, ivory racemes. In mid spring clustered florets of typical pea-blossom shape drape from its highest branches. These recall the sweet-scented panicles of black locust (*Robinia pseudoacacia*), itself a beautiful leguminous tree, lovely in blossom and memorable in honey-rich fragrance. Although prone to suckering and short lived, black locust warrants a place in a moonlight display. When happily positioned, it will smother in creamy flowers each spring, reblooming periodically through summer. Both this and yellowwood adapt to a variety of garden soils and situations.

The curious feathery white blooms of the granddaddy graybeard or fringe tree (*Chionanthus virginicus*) have won the hearts of several generations of gardeners. On the acid soils of the Southeast, where this vanilla-scented cousin of the lilac is a native, it is one of the most popular spring-flowering trees. Where soils are limy or alkaline, the Chinese fringe tree (*Chionanthus retusus*) makes a fine substitute, with similar panicles of creamy froth against dark waxy foliage.

Each spring the pristine eastern dogwoods (*Cornus florida*) fill forest understories with lilting horizontal branches topped in fat crosses of parchment white; where these elegant natives succeed, few flowering trees illuminate a wood more effectively. If garden earths contains a measure of lime, however, Chinese dogwood (*Cornus kousa* v. *chinensis*) and Mexican dogwood (*Cornus urbaniana*) are the varieties to try, for these robust trees tolerate mild alkalinity. Though less dramatic than eastern dogwood, both the Chinese and the Mexican species are worth having; their distinctive blooms resemble four-petaled ivory stars and quaintly cupped creamy lanterns, respectively.

In the South and throughout the prairie states, the varied hawthorns or mayhaws (*Crataegus* spp.) , wild plums (*Prunus* spp.), and native crabapples (*Malus* spp.) erupt in clouds of pale blossom each spring. The cream or light-pink flowers offer pleasant visual additions in a moonlight garden and each of these genera provides distinctive fragrances to add to the night: thick and cloying for hawthorn; sweet and overpowering for plum; light and refreshing for crabapple.

These small trees also nourish a gentle droning sound through their blooming seasons, for they attract hoards of insects. Even at night butterflies, skippers, and other nectar-hungry creatures will be seen as silhouettes before the pale clustered blossoms. In summer and autumn ripening amber fruits will show in the night as pleasantly as the spring flowers.

Woodland Shrubs

Just beneath these understory trees, a universe of shade-loving woody plants awaits the exploration of gardeners. The most beloved in the South are hybrid azaleas (*Rhododendron* cvs.), famed for their iridescent floral displays in early spring. Any of the white or pale-flowered sorts show handsomely at night, so they might be included in nocturnal schemes, although most of the year the twiggy shrubs constitute simple masses of dark foliage. A varied array of ever-green azalea cultivars can be grown easily in the wooded South, offering massed flowers in spring and scattering blooms through the rest of the year. Moist shaded beds filled with acid, humus-rich soils like peat moss or partly decayed pine bark are their only requirements.

More intriguing for night gardens are several deciduous azaleas with long-tubed flowers that are pleasantly fragrant. The hoary azalea or wild honeysuckle (*Rhododendron canescens*) disposes clusters of blushed white heliotrope-scented blossoms among its gracefully layered branches from March into May. Long pink stamens project beyond the petals, a sure sign that these flowers are out to attract hummingbirds and butterflies for pollination. Nevertheless, early season hawkmoths also find the sweet blossoms attractive, and it comes as no surprise to see one of these nighttime insects hovering over the orchidlike blooms with its slender proboscis artfully bent and inserted for a sip.

Florida flame azalea (*Rhododendron austrinum*) is even more arresting, with clustered spidery trusses that vary from straw and amber through all the warm tones of yellow, gold, and orange. The exotic blossoms glow in moonlight and reveal the gaunt, open habits of these three- to four-foot bushes that grow taller than wide. The same well-drained soils that favor dogwoods provide homes for these aristocratic natives of Georgia and northern Florida. *Rhododendron alabamense*, *R. arborescens*, *R. atlanticum*, and the Choptank hybrids are other useful native azaleas with pale, fragrant blooms that may be encouraged to naturalize under pines in the South.

Gardeners with tight clay or alkaline soil will need to make special provisions for these, or any azaleas, if they are to succeed. Yet, even in gardens built over limestone, a fairly permanent situation for these finicky shrubs might be arranged in association with a shaded garden pool. A small rock-based island or peninsula could be built into the pond to make nooks for these favored shrubs. Beds of peat or pine bark blended with acid minerals such as decomposed granite or basalt can then be mounded above the water line to construct a special azalea island. This special friable soil will wick moisture to the shrubs without becoming soggy and sustain acid-loving azaleas, hydrangeas, and camellias even in regions where soils and waters are limy and alkaline.

The lopsided greenish white clusters of the oakleaf hydrangeas (*Hydrangea quercifolia*) begin looming out of the forest shadows in May. With their massive and distinctive forms, these are among the most obvious blooms in moonlight, doubly so for their refreshing light fragrance. The handsome shrubs reach six feet or more, with coarsely lobed green foliage to set a stark background for the flowers. Although these deciduous natives prefer rich acid soils, they usually succeed on any ground that remains unfailingly damp.

Another shrub of special beauty, *Hydrangea macrophylla* 'Tricolor' earns a place in the nocturnal composition not for its lacecap flowers (which appear rarely, if at all, in southern gardens), but for its unmistakable variegated foliage. Crisply serrated dark green leaves marble with cream and light mint, creating a pattern that seems, like a firefly, simultaneously cool and luminous. As with the oakleaf hydrangeas, these two-foot mounding shrubs succeed in damp shade almost anywhere.

Ordinary yellow-dusted strains of Japanese aucuba (*Aucuba japonica*) are too mildly variegated to be of much value at night, but the gold-centered 'Picturata' and butter-margined 'Sulfur' seem bright enough to show even on moonless nights. These slow-growing evergreens are easily accommodated in any thoroughly shaded bed and are hardy through the South. They would be ideal for planting near a wooded path where some extra night-lighting was needed to keep wanderers on track on gloomy evenings.

Spicebush (*Lindera Benzoin*), with pale spring flowers, aromatic leaves, and clear yellow fall foliage, sweet box (*Sarcococca ruscifolia*), with darkly spreading evergreen branches and tiny sweet-scented spring blooms, and Japanese glory-bower (*Clerodendrum trichotomum*), with starry white summer flowers followed by turquoise berries, are additional subjects for the nocturnal woodland understory. All are easy growing in the South.

Moonlit Bowers

In many parts of the eastern U.S., native woodlands have been choked and devoured by a rough invader. What was once a diverse wilderness has been conquered, forcibly unified in a spreading empire of velvety green tendrils. Yet, with the humid atmosphere of dusk, this ecological disaster finds redemption. Indigenous vegetation may be a memory, but the sweet fragrance of that most characteristically Southern vine, the honeysuckle, wafts gently through the summer air.

Although it has made itself at home in America for over a century and may now be counted a permanent member of our flora, the Japanese honeysuckle (*Lonicera japonica*) is originally native to scrub and woodland of China, Japan, and Korea. Its creamy flowers emit a powerful scent on summer evenings, fading to amber as they age on their second day. These familiar silver and gold clusters may be seen in dooryards and byways throughout North America, and as a rite of passage every child learns how to pluck the slender pistils from the tubular blossoms so that the fat drops of nectar can be extracted and sipped.

Japanese honeysuckle is a true night flower. As dusk approaches, the straplike, united petals fold backwards and upwards to open the clustered tubular throats of the slender blooms. Hawkmoths descend eagerly and fragrance drifts sweetly through the evening air. No other hardy vine displays such obvious nocturnal habits.

Honeysuckles may be trained as scrambling shrubs, as vines, or as ground covers and perform admirably in all these roles. 'Purpurea' is a selection that sets off its purple-tinged blooms with dark-toned foliage; 'Hall's' is the popular green leafed form of the species with all-white flowers and overpowering vigor. Although tolerant of shade, the fragrant blossoms appear more abundantly in sunlight. For woodland gardens, these vines are best at forest's edge where the evergreen foliage can sprawl to provide enclosure and the sun can encourage the sensuous evening blossoms.

There is a native honeysuckle in the South, a handsome scarlet climber called coral honeysuckle (*Lonicera sempervirens*). In its ordinary reddish phase this unscented vine has little to offer a night garden, but the yellow cultivar, 'Sulphurea', is quite effective in moonlight and provides a well-behaved climber ideal for training up posts or over the branches of a willing tree. Its long-tubed primrose flowers appear from March to October and need only a dim illumination to excite and enhance their natural glow. The warm yellow variant of the native trumpet creeper, *Campsis radicans* 'Flava' is similarly lovely at night but too aggressive to be trusted in a small garden.

Another famously fragrant vine of the South, the Carolina jessamine (*Gelsemium sempervirens*), might be included among the winter flowers, for at least some of its yellow blooms appear in the coldest months of the year. Although valuable for this habit, these native climbers hold their real displays for spring, when the glossy evergreen leaves smother in clouds of butter yellow bells. The powerful scent of these honey-toned blooms overwhelms the crispness of the early season so that even this moment of the year seems like a sultry evening spent among tropical flowers.

There is a small early-season hawkmoth that usually visits the tubular blossoms. Their blurred wings may be seen passing before the pale flowers near dusk and early in the morning, and one supposes that they are after the jessamine all night. These beautiful blooms must be hard for the insects to resist, for when in full display the draping masses seem as sulfury as the moon itself.

With its neat evergreen habit, Carolina jessamine is one of the most

Mexican plum, *Prunus mexicana*

A woodland aster, *Aster texanus*

Fragrant plantain lily, *Hosta* 'Royal Standard'

Southern magnolia, *Magnolia grandiflora*

Japanese honeysuckle, *Lonicera japonica* 'Halliana' (Greg Grant)

popular vines in the nursery trade and seems to grows easily on any damp soil. In the wild the vines inhabit swampy woodlands. Although these twining evergreens can be short lived on heavy clays and on dry soils, they are still worth growing for their fragrance and will climb happily on any slender support. Replacements grow quickly, so a few young plants can be kept coming along for the day when the veterans give up the contest. Like honeysuckle, Carolina jessamine tolerates shade but blooms more profusely where its draping stems capture the sun. A double-flowered selection, 'Pride of Augusta', is offered by a few growers; at night this would hardly be separable from the common sort, but it may appeal to gardeners who enjoy an extra measure of artifice.

This golden climber finds its natural complement in the pale lavender-blue of Chinese wisteria (*Wisteria sinensis*), a rampant vine of gardens that seems to be growing half-wild even when restrained to an arbor, fence, or post. The drooping scented pea-flowers are a common sight smothering tall trees in April. Few vines make a more romantic or successful addition to an established woodland.

Although by no means nighttime flowers, the rich fragrance of wisteria is strong in the evening, and if the white form, 'Alba', can be had, then the flowers can show in the darkness as well. It is important in the South to make sure the Chinese species is selected rather than the Japanese (*Wisteria floribunda*), for the latter blooms shyly in warm climates. It is a good rule, also, to buy only flowering plants of any wisteria, since inferior nonblooming stock might otherwise take years to blossom. Although entirely deciduous and bare through the winter months, a good wisteria vine will regularly disappear in blossom in early spring and provide occasional off-season flowers the rest of the summer.

Late in the summer the panicled sweet-autumn clematis (*Clematis dioscoreifolia*) drapes a fragrant white veneer over its rambling tents of leathery green, making a show in the most dim illumination. This reliable vine might be trained along the edges of a wood so that its fall blooms, and the feathery seeds that follow, could ramble among the understory. Although the best flowers come on stems that lie in direct sun, shade otherwise suits this fragrant vine, which commonly persists in the neglected corners of older gardens. Its masses of silvery four-petaled blooms are never better than in the clear light of an autumn moon.

The Forest in Spring

Most of the herbaceous layer of the forest blooms early in the year, for this allows these lowly plants to complete growth before the shaded canopy fills with leaves. So-called "spring ephemerals" leaf out in late winter, flower in earliest spring, and then disappear or sleep peacefully as simple carpets of greenery for the rest of the summer.

The snow poppy (*Eomecon chionantha*) typifies this early routine, sending up leafy patches of rounded, wavy-edged leaves and short stems carrying several white four-petaled blooms. The pale lighting of early spring moons captures the pristine beauty of these simple flowers, which, like magnolias, are among the most primitively constructed blossoms.

Rich orange-red sap, similar to that of its famous American cousin the bloodroot (*Sanguinaria canadensis*), flows in the stems of this curious oriental perennial. As a garden flower, the snow poppy is more robust than its western hemisphere kin and will spread rapidly over the forest floor, creating lush pools of greenery. Although the blooms appear primarily in spring, it is not unusual to see a few late flowers among the massed leaves as summer progresses.

Yellowish-orange sap and four-petaled blossoms show up in another genus of Asian woodlanders, the bishop's hats (*Epimedium* spp.). With their curiously divided evergreen foliage, these low plants are invaluable for carpeting deep humus-laden soils under oaks and other hardwoods. Hatlike or cup-and-saucer shaped blooms appear quietly above the handsome leaves in early spring. For night gardens, the white *Epimedium* x *youngianum* 'Yamamoto Form' and the acid yellow *E.* x *versicolor* 'Neosulphureum' would be choice. These cultivars are among the easiest growing of the bishop's hats and provide excellent ground cover for gardens in the middle and upper South.

Although *Epimedium* belongs to the barberry family (*Berberidaceae*) rather than the poppy family (*Papaveraceae*), its resemblance to the snow poppy is not accidental. Bishop's hats are the rightful allies of these, of bloodroots, and of the other woodland flora in the barberry, poppy, and anemone families (*Ranunculaceae*). These primordial understory plants all arrived early in the evolution of flowers, and they share many characteristics along with their preferences for moist, shaded environments.

The gentle lobing and division of foliage common to the early woodlanders seems to reiterate in the gracefully parted leaves of the rue anemone (*Anemonella thalictroides*), one of the most refined and beautiful of North American wildflowers. Deceptively delicate in appearance, this tuberous rooted perennial proves among the most robust garden flowers, with a hardy constitution that belies its immaculate white florets. These appear in small groups centered among the foliage and bear five to ten rounded white sepals around a boss of yellowish stamens.

In blossom design, the rue anemone recalls the true anemones, which include several valuable flowers for woodland. The best in the South are the wood anemone (*Anemone nemorosa*) and the Japanese anemone (*Anemone* x *hybrida*).

The first is a dwarfish plant with rambling stems, deeply cut foliage, and modest white flowers that appear in spring and again in fall. Although too thinly furnished with leaves to perform as a ground cover, the wood anemone is a steadfast bloomer and grows easily from tuberous divisions. These may be set at various points through the woodland to spread their charming blossoms.

The well-loved Japanese anemones sport poppylike flowers that break anemone tradition by coming in the fall rather than in the spring. Thick maplelike foliage provides cover and is useful as a weed smotherer all summer, turning to russet tones in the fall. Under moonlight the famous white-flowered selection of 1858, 'Honorine Jobert', seems difficult to surpass, with eighteen-inch stems topped by yellow-centered blooms over several weeks of autumn, but other Japanese anemones in pale pink shades are also suitable candidates for wooded gardens in the middle and upper South.

Along with these, the hybrid strains of the leafy evergreen Lenten roses (*Helleborus orientalis*), especially the forms with dappled pink, pale yellow, white, or chartreuse blossoms, may be allowed to seed themselves and carpet the forest. These cousins of the anemones retain a somber appearance even in daylight, but under the moon their many-parted leaves glisten magically, so that any wood that contains them seems to be enchanted. Although not easy to grow in the drier, hotter Southwest and Gulf regions, in the mid South these hardy perennials are among the best and easiest flowers, growing well in moist soils with a measure of lime. Other hellebores such as Christmas rose (*Helleborus niger*), stinking hellebore (*H. foetidus*), and Corsican hellebore (*H. lividus corsicus*) are less certain performers but are worth trying in cool woodlands for their distinctively lobed, finger-shaped foliage.

Although entirely distinct from these showy flowers, the odd meadow rues (*Thalictrum* spp.) reveal kinship to the rue anemone in their ferny, divided foliage. In most species the leaves are a lush bluish tone that reads as metallic gray on a moonlit night. This affords a hushed contrast to the feathery blossoms, comprised entirely of clustered stamens. *Thalictrum aquilegifolium*, with fluffy clumps of lilac pink, and *T. delavyi*, with graceful branches bearing creamy puffs, are the two most commonly planted species. These quietly beautiful plants reach two feet in height, forming regal pyramids of airy foliage and flowers. Both have good white forms suited to nocturnal display that share the cultivar name, 'Album', and grow easily in any shaded position with deep soil.

The many-parted foliage of the noble *Thalictrum* shows up again in the columbines (*Aquilegia* spp.), beloved for their fairylike, spurred blossoms. Although the common native species of the South, *Aquilegia canadensis*, is a true woodlander and a valuable, strong-growing perennial, its coppery blossoms have been structured to attract hummingbirds and offer a poor show at night.

For the moon garden, it is the yellow columbines of the Southwest that offer evening performances, attracting the night-flying hawkmoths that come early in the year. *Aquilegia chrysantha* and its west Texas variety, *hinckleyana*, are the best of these pale species, with beautiful primrose blossoms above dense clumps of blue-green foliage in April. Although native to streamsides and springs in the uplands of the Southwest, these stocky perennials seem to do well in gardens everywhere. They enjoy well-drained, root-filled soils under mature trees and will often self sow and naturalize in southern woodlands. When these golden flowers come to full spring display, they have few rivals for beauty, especially at night.

The long-spurred columbine (*Aquilegia longissima*) blooms after the other yellow species, sometimes as late as July. Its overendowed sulfury blooms carry disproportionately long spurs that give the small plants an otherworldly attraction. Hovering hawkmoths and occasional hummingbirds come to sip from these peculiar tubular nectaries and do a fine job of pollinating the columbines. Seed of all the species ripens just a month after flowering and in autumn can be planted in gritty soil directly where plants are desired. Only two seasons of growth are needed to develop full-sized columbines, which will flower for years thereafter.

To further enhance the whiteness of the nocturnal spring, the snowy Naples onion (*Allium neapolitanum*) might be allowed to spread and seed itself through the woodland. These early flowers are among the purest and appear amid the light green, garlicky leaves at a very tender moment of spring. One of the easiest bulbs to grow in the deciduous woodlands of the middle and lower South, this naturalizing species is a half-hardy native of southern Europe.

Slightly later flowering and more tolerant of cold, the white forms of Spanish bluebell (*Endymion hispanicus*) might spread their carpets of upright clustered bloom among the nocturnal forest. These bulbs of the lily family are allies of the squills (*Scilla* spp.); they multiply rapidly by both seed and offsets on moist, sandy soils.

The native Atamasco lily (*Zephyranthes atamasco*) also enjoys such damp positions, sending up its white lily-scented funnels around Easter. These fragrant blooms are big enough to count on dark nights and are true evening flowers meant for the moths. Atamascos will naturalize on acid forest soils, making useful clumps to set at the foot of leafy shrubs or darkly mossy tree trunks.

With them, the white Japanese roof iris (*Iris tectorum* 'Album') could be allowed to develop large patches along the forest paths. These substantial flowers, like pale orchids, will light the woods with reflected moonglow. Japanese evergreen iris (*Iris japonica*) and its subtropic hybrid, 'Nada', might be invited into the nocturnal woodlands as well. Although their pale spring flowers are smaller than those of *I. tectorum*, they appear in ethereal sprays above the gracefully arched swords of foliage. 'Nada' performs best in the frost-sheltered gardens of the lower South, but *I. tectorum* and *I. japonica* accept a measure of cold and can be counted hardy at least through the middle South; both have vibrant variegated forms that deserve special attention in night plantings.

Among these irises, a few pale blossoms of the true hardy orchid, *Bletilla striata* 'Alba', would make an enchanting nocturnal scene and might be tucked in any convenient shaded nook. The delicately cupped blooms appear in April among the lush patches of tongue-shaped leaves and, though small, are effective in lighting a dim wood. The bifurcating tubers of the orchid seem to grow well in any moist soil and prove thoroughly hardy in the South if mulched occasionally with a layer of fallen leaves.

On rougher, drier sites in the woods some of the pale-flowered early daisies might be added for their luminous starry heads of bloom. The thin white ray-flowers of Philadelphia fleabane (*Erigeron philadelphicus*) surround small yellow disks, creating slender sprays of fluffy composite blossoms like white asters. In cool climates these native perennials flower in the summer sun, but in the South they enjoy shade and bloom earlier, in mid-spring. A few patches of these wildflowers set about the woods gives an eerie glow to a moonlit forest.

Even brighter, the golden groundsel (*Senecio obovatus*) contrasts dainty yellow daisies with black-green, paddle-shaped foliage. This wild daisy recalls the robust Ligularia cultivars of temperate European gardens, though on a more modest foot-high scale. Its evergreen leaves form a lush forest carpet that withstands drought as well as dampness, making this unassuming native plant one of the most useful spring perennials.

Carpeters and Illuminators

The natural floor of the forest fills with slow-growing grassy plants, usually in varying tones of darkest green. Sedge (*Carex* spp.), monkey grass (*Liriope* spp.), mondo grass (*Ophiopogon* spp.), and Japanese flag (*Acorus* cvs.) are the grasslike perennials common to understory plantings in the South. Although these evergreens are normally provided with dark-toned foliage, even the blackest of the sedges has enough shininess in its leaves to reflect moonglow, and each of these genera includes white-flowered or variegated representatives of value at night.

The best of the sedges, *Carex hachioensis* 'Evergold' is an old Oriental selection with bright ivory-striped leaves that make pale tussocks on the forest floor. In many nursery lists, this centrally striped form is called by an old synonym, *Carex morrowii* 'Aureo Variegata', and it is sometimes referred to as 'Old Gold' or 'Everbrite'. Although the strongly colored foliage suffers in hot sun, these plants are not otherwise difficult to grow under moist, shady conditions. The glowing variegation of 'Evergold' surpasses that of the commoner silver-edged Japanese sedge (*Carex morrowii* 'Goldband') and makes a strong statement for any nocturnal garden.

The white-flowered forms of *Liriope spicata,* such as 'Monroe White', also offer good choices for night plantings, rambling freely through the forest with spreading underground stems. Short spikes of tiny lily-bells appear among the dark tufts of foliage in late spring. Although the evergreen leaves flatten in winter, disappearing under cover of autumn leaves, they return vigorously each spring.

An arresting white-variegated selection, 'Silver Dragon', is even more exciting and much better than the old *Liriope muscari* form, 'Silvery Sunproof'. Since 'Silver Dragon' spreads by questing roots like all the *spicata* forms, after a few seasons it forms large patches. At night these look like pools of pale water and, with strategic positioning, will guide visitors through the gloom even on moonless nights. As with other *spicata* selections, 'Silver Dragon' lays down and disappears under the forest leaves for winter, but its spring return, like hundreds of small white fountains, is a moment to be cherished. A subtropical variant of giant liriope known as Aztec grass and usually listed under the name *Ophiopogon jaburan* 'Variegatus' is a larger evergreen cousin of these cream-striped liriopes, valuable for shaded beds in the lower South.

Ophiopogon also includes useful white-flowered forms, especially the black-leafed *Ophiopogon planiscapus* 'Nigrescens'. This dark variant, as well as the ordinary green form of the species, makes good slowly rambling ground cover useful as contrast for lighter leaved plants or stones. The white blooms, sometimes tinged with pink, appear in late spring and later ripen to dull blue-green berries.

Cultivars of the grassy Japanese sweet flag (*Acorus gramineus*) show a definite preference for damp conditions, thriving even as aquatics. Nevertheless, these odd members of the arum family (*Araceae)* adapt to almost any moist, shaded bed. Their common name refers to a sweet essence obtained from the roots of the larger water-loving *Acorus calamus*.

As valued as they may be, the clustered eight-inch fans of the cream-striped *Acorus gramineus* 'Variegatus' pale before the glowing gold-toned selection 'Ogon'. With their upswept tapered leaves, both are valuable to associate with boulders or other strong shapes. For planting in moist crevices between stones, the bleached chartreuse tufts of the diminutive 'Pusillus Minimus Aureus' are unsurpassed.

Along with these thin-leaved carpeters, some heftier variegated subjects can be set in dark corners of the forest to make the most of the moonbeams. The silver-etched leaves of the Japanese Solomon's-seal (*Polygonatum falcatum* 'Variegata') stand out boldly from its reddish stems so that at night the ovate leaflets seem to be floating in the darkness. This hardy two- to three-foot perennial is another member of the lily family and, like the liriopes, carries small, pendant, white bells along its flowering stems.

Best known of all the woodland lily tribe, especially for their supremely variegated leaves, are the oriental plantain lilies, or hostas. These hardy perennials are standard fare in any temperate garden and they even have fans in the lower South, although their performance in warm regions is erratic at best. There are no finer foliage plants anywhere, and where these cool-climate perennials succeed, the nocturnal garden can have its fill of fine variegations, both cream and gold, displayed on the most textural of leafy rosettes.

Hostas also produce pale lavender-toned flowers that are of value at night, and at least one species, *H. plantaginea*, offers true fragrant night flowers for the moths. These are slightly tubular white bells that come on long stems in midsummer after most of the other hostas have finished their season. Although quite hardy, this night-flowering variant is the most adaptable type for warm regions, growing farther south in China than the other common garden species, which are natives of Japan and Korea.

Since they are fragrant, breeders have added many new hybrids and selections of *H. plantaginea*. Nurseries are making these night flowers more and more readily available through tissue culture propagation, so formerly expensive novelties may now be had at little cost. Some cultivars with especially large, fragrant blooms for nocturnal display include 'Grandiflora', 'Royal Standard', and 'Honeybells'. 'Sum and Substance', with huge rosettes of greenish yellow foliage, 'Aphrodite', with double white blooms, and 'Sugar and Cream', with fragrant blooms and creamy variegated leaves, are choice. All of these cultivars thrive on moist, shaded ground and bear tall spikes of sweet-scented flowers in midsummer. Mulches of pine straw or other prickly bedding may help deter slugs and snails if such pests are a continuing threat.

The list of variegated carpeters suited to general woodland gardens includes other old favorites such as dead nettle (*Lamium maculatum* 'Variegatum'), with crimped silver leaflets distributed along aggressively trailing stems, and the adaptable bishop's weed (*Aegopodium podagraria*

'Variegatum'), with coarsely divided leaflets edged in cream like oddly luminous parsley. Both are easy growers on moist soil. The Japanese silver fern (*Athyrium nipponicum* 'Pictum') is another moisture-loving subject worthwhile at night for its feathery platinum-stained fronds. Apparently as hardy as our native ferns, this elegant species does well through most of the South.

On drier ground, the winter-growing *Vinca major* 'Variegata' makes a thrifty spreader, with pale-toned leaves and light-blue blossoms in midspring. This is an aggressive ground cover and, like the ivies (*Hedera* spp.), should be restrained, lest it take the whole forest. Of the many ivy cultivars, the most valuable at night are those with reflective or pale-toned leaves, although all make excellent ground covers and good subjects to train on walls or up the stems of trees.

In the lower South, the shiny heart-shaped leaves of the half-hardy Algerian ivy (*Hedera algeriensis*) reflect moonlight through the woods, while its creamy-marbled form, 'Gloire de Marengo', wholly absorbs lunar light, radiating back a warm glow. Elsewhere the variegated forms of English ivy (*Hedera helix*) are hardy and worth adding to night plantings; they are not so aggressive as the green forms of the plant and so may be allowed to sprawl at the base of mossy stones where their bright leaves will show to advantage. The grayed blue *Hedera nepalensis* seems almost too ghostly to add to a night garden, but the dark veins of its leaflets provide just the contrast needed to show off its curiously patterned foliage.

To create a glowing patch of gold on the forest floor, the ornamental oregano *Origanum vulgare* 'Norton's Golden' is an adaptable choice. Although lush and leafy at all times, this hardy evergreen herb will accept very dry conditions, so it's a good performer under trees like oaks that aggressively wick moisture from the soil in summer. The aromatic chartreuse foliage lies usefully flat on the ground, making a nice contrast to stones or to dark-leaved perennials.

As with any night garden, in the forest it is this contrast of light and dark that makes plantings come alive. To enhance their value, these light-toned foliage plants might be combined with such shade lovers as the brownish purple *Heuchera micrantha* 'Palace Purple'. These popular perennials have an almost metallic sheen to their rosettes of maplelike leaves. At night they afford an effective blackness to show off good golds and silvers.

Summer and Autumn Flowers

As summer progresses, a variety of flowering plants will emerge from the leafy masses of the understory to take their turns under the moon. The most noble are the trumpet lilies whose creamy blossoms have been fashioned to attract the night moths. The sweet-scented Bermuda lily *(Lilium longiflorum* v. *eximium)* is the first of these, with flowers arriving in March. These are followed by the pink-tinged regal lilies *(Lilium regale)* with their butter-toned throats and by the whole royal court of amber and yellow-toned Olympic and Aurelian hybrids descended from these and other night-flowering lilies of the Orient.

In the South, the most dependable and last to flower is the Philippine lily *(Lilium formosanum)*, which usually puts in an appearance in July. Its sweet-scented drooping trumpets look much like the Easter lilies of spring but have a more slender bearing. In many gardens these old-fashioned flowers seed themselves through the woods, so that their rising stems move about the garden, coming as a surprise each season.

Although not entirely hardy, the white globes of *Agapanthus orientalis* 'Alba' are so handsome in moonlight that they are worth bedding out from time to time. The umbels of pale campanulate blooms rise from lush clumps of strapping leaves and appear for many weeks of summer. These moisture-loving perennials need protection from severe cold and demand well-drained soil in the winter, but they are otherwise easy growing.

In the South, the late summer is also the time for the subtropical cousins of amaryllis called spider lilies, or hurricane lilies. These belong to the Oriental genus *Lycoris* and include several species and hybrids. For moonlight the best are the yellow *Lycoris africana* and *L. traubii* and the creamy *L. albiflora*. All grow easily in the lower South, asking only for a bit of the forest where they will not be disturbed. With fall rains the feathery blooms arrive atop slender naked stems, looking like amazing orchids set among the woods. Afterwards the bulbs send up their wintertime foliage.

Another plant often though of as exotic also has a white-flowered variant suited to night gardens. The hardy begonia *(Begonia grandis* 'Alba') makes towers of handsome red-veined foliage bearing crystalline white blooms over most of the summer. This Chinese species grows from tubers and multiplies rapidly in gardens to its liking; constant moisture and shelter from hot sun are its only demands. It makes an ethereal nighttime scene by a shaded pile of boulders or a fern-covered ledge.

This would also be a good place to show off the strange habits of the toad lilies *(Tricyrtis* spp.). At least one of these hardy oriental woodlanders, a selection called 'White Towers', has blooms pale enough to count under the moon. These starlike flowers appear along the tops of the gently curved stems, which spread in patches on moist ground.

In drier spaces, the white mountain mint *(Pycnanthemum albescens)* makes drifts of small pointed leaves topped in summer by ghostly white bracts and tiny blossoms. The dim glow of this foliage offers an invitation to brush near, releasing its powerfully refreshing pennyroyal scent.

A distinctive woodland daisy, *Vigethia mexicana* recalls the pale flowers of leopard bane with narrow yellow rays surrounding a chartreuse disk. These sizable blossoms appear among the half-woody stems and large felted leaves from spring through summer. Although at three feet this lax perennial seems to straggle at times, it manages an air of nobility unusual for a daisy.

Texas asters (*Aster texanus*) and heart-leaf asters (*A. cordifolia*) are more typical of the composite family, with rank vigor producing clouds of small pale lavender daisies in delicate sprays. These woodland plants overwinter as rosettes of heart-shaped leaves and accept both wet and modestly dry soils. Their graceful, softly colored blooms light up shady corners in late October and afford a welcome station for south-migrating butterflies.

On dry ground these insects feast instead on the flowers of boneset (*Eupatorium havanense*) and frostweed (*Verbesina virginica*), woodland representatives of the daisy tribe especially equipped for dry positions. The first is a half-hardy evergreen shrublet with snowy powderpuff blooms in late autumn, an ideal plant to set among crevices in a shaded stone wall. The second is a rank perennial, clothed in tobaccolike leaves and annually redeemed by plates of flat white florets. Although rather ordinary in the day, both the boneset and the frostweed offer the necessary contrast and texture to show beautifully in moonlight.

Deadfall

With this in mind, it is well to remember that overly tidy gardening may fail to see much of the beauty in a space. Stones and tree trunks will become darker and more ominous if we let them cover with mosses, creating pools of black in the woods. Ferns left to ramble in low spaces will provide a feathery blur of gray to enclose the garden at night and make visitors feel welcome. Throughout the woods the half-rotted branches and decaying stumps of trees can be left like the bones of some ancient titan, evidence of the age and majesty of the forest. Perhaps the creamy oyster fungus (*Pleurotus ostreatus*) will even start to grow on these rotting timbers and on some very special nights the eerie glow of fluorescent Jack-o-Lantern mushrooms will be sighted deep in the dark.

If the prairie be small, its greatest beauty consists in the vicinity of the surrounding margin of woodland, which resembles the shore of a lake, indented with deep vistas, like bays and inlets, and throwing out long points, like capes and headlands; while occasionally these points approach so close on either hand, that the traveller passes through a narrow avenue, or strait, where the shadows of woodland fall on his path, and then again emerges into another prairie.

JAMES HALL, STATISTICS OF THE WEST AT THE CLOSE OF THE YEAR, 1836

FOUR

The Prairie Moon

pportunities to view prairies in anything like an undisturbed state are today uncommon, yet visitors to these magnificent natural places still share a profound reaction. The rolling landscape, with its open swells of grasses and flowers, scattered clumps of trees, and overarching dome of sky, invokes descriptives usually reserved for the ocean. These gently undulating territories appear at once vast and embracing. Like the primordial sea, prairies touch a deep point of the human spirit.

When viewed in the half light of the moon, this elemental landscape loses none of its power, for the patterns of light and dark, mass and void, become even more apparent. On a more intimate scale, diverse grasses and flowers flow around the wanderer as a brocade of textures. This splendid world includes myriad nocturnal blossoms, insects, and other varied creatures who fill the prairie nights with fragrance, sound, and intrigue.

A Prairie Plot

To bring something of the grandeur of this landscape to a small garden, plantings might be laid out around an irregular lawn or short grassed meadow. This could be surrounded by thicketed trees, shrubs, perennial flowers, and taller grasses to create a small naturalistic enclosure. Although ordinary mowed turf might suffice for the central open space, a less manicured surface of native grass would help create the illusion of a larger scale and would be more in keeping with the coarse, wild spirit of the prairie. In the softness of moonlight pale, wispy tufts of buffalo grass (*Buchloe dactyloides*) and blue grama (*Bouteloua gracilis*) could be mixed to create a miniature silvery meadow.

These short grasses thrive over most of central North America and need little attention once they have established in open sun. Most such native "lawns" only want mowing once or twice a year and will be less bothered by weeds and other problems if they are left unfertilized and unirrigated. Since these grasses do not ordinarily make a thick cover, they leave room for wild-flowers, which may be allowed to complete their cycle of bloom and seed production before being cut down in early summer. Where denser grass is appropriate, a select buffalo grass called '609' might be employed; this Nebraska variety has a blue-green color ideal for a night garden.

The winter color of these grasses is another of their assets. The strawlike tones of December reflect moonbeams even more warmly than the August dress of gray-blue. Both buffalo grass and blue grama are also notable for their capacity to harvest the evening dews. At night the slender leaves capture moisture on small hairs distributed along the blades, so that by morning the whole lawn covers in tiny silvery drops. These give a ghostly cast to the grasses at night, effectively lighting the garden.

Since blue grama is a clumping grass and buffalo grass spreads only by surface runners, neither become invasive. Beds surrounding the miniature meadow might be edged with simple lines of stones or by maintaining a short moat between the turf and its surroundings, clumping grasses and perennials encroaching to create the illusion of a wild, rugged section of grassland.

A Poem of Light and Dark

As an entry to this artificial glade, a series of columnar masonry posts might be set to support an arbor or glorietta planted to mustang grape (*Vitis cinerea*). This rampant prairie climber can be seen smothering the scrubby oaks and elms that dot the frontier, draped in late summer (on the female vines) with loose clusters of tart black berries. In gardens the mustang grape displays a quiet beauty that comes mostly from dark green maple-shaped foliage. This is coated with a whitish felt on its underside, and this same silver material appears on the new shoots. This jumble of light and dark leaves above a few thick, ghostly columns would be a moving entryway into the nocturnal prairie realm.

Motts

Spanish colonists on the Southwestern prairies encountered scattered clumps, or *mota*, made by the small, crooked trees growing among the grasses. The harsh climate, with its desiccating winds and irregular rainfall, made life rough for these trees, which invariably responded by growing as multi-stemmed thickets. Although the trees lacked the noble symmetry of their woodland cousins, they evoked the power of their terrain in gnarled stems and twisted trunks.

For a romantic garden effect, several irregular trees might be grouped around the central meadow to suggest a prairie copse. These clumps, or "motts," could be made from any of the native oaks or elms, whose dark foliage and heavy stems might lend a rugged blackness to the evening garden. Upright junipers such as the eastern red cedar (*Juniperus virginiana*) might be added to this perimeter as well for their distinctive pyramidal silhouettes.

To give height and to add a gentle rustling to the evening, a few cotton-woods or poplars might be set along one edge. These fast-growing trees remain eternally thirsty if planted away from their native streambanks, yet they prove surprisingly drought tolerant when established. It is also true that the heart-shaped leaves of poplars shed through the summer and demand continual rak-ing, yet no other hardy plant offers the softly moving leafy tower of a cottonwood. This murmuring foliage, twisting endlessly in the prairie breezes, adds a countermelody to the evening songs of crickets, katydids, and the cho-rus of frogs and toads that follow the summer showers. As fall approaches, these most typical prairie trees are among the first to turn to gold.

For the nocturnal garden, any of the "cottonless" male selections of cot-tonwoods or poplars would be rewarding; the large-leafed eastern cottonwood (*Populus deltoides*) is one that has proven hardy in many gardens. Although it suckers fiercely and usually inclines its trunk with the prevailing wind, the sil-ver poplar (*Populus alba*) would be worth considering for its white bark and silver-backed leaves. In a small yard its upright form, 'Bolleana', might be used to create a silver screen against the night sky. Although these soft-wooded poplars can be short lived, they grow rapidly from cuttings taken in the dor-mant season and placed directly into well-drained garden soil.

Other rugged trees such as box elder (*Acer negundo*), black walnut (*Juglans nigra*), and bois d'arc (*Maclura pomifera*) might be included along the perimeter to give evening roosts for droning cicadas and coarse leaves to turn gold with the autumn frosts. Such hardy exotics as goldenrain tree (*Koelreuteria paniculata*) and tree of heaven (*Ailanthus altissima*) might add ferny foliage and luminous seed clusters to the nocturnal scene. Even more telling, the supple bowers of Russian olive (*Elaeagnus angustifolia*) could fill

Shrubby boneset, *Eupatorium havanense*
(Paul Cox)

Wild foxglove, *Penstemon cobaea* (Paul
Cox)

Prairie blazing star, *Mentzelia decapetala*
(Paul Cox)

Giant prairie lily,
Zephyranthes drummondii

voids left in the plantings with silver-gray leaves as their minute yellowish blossoms imbue the evening breezes with a honeyed aroma.

If there is room, space might be allocated for a pecan. These denizens of the South and Southwest are the bane of suburban gardeners, cursed for their messy leaves, broken branches, and attraction to insects. Yet, at night the exuberant pecan reveals itself as a prince of the prairie. The canopy of pinnately dissected leaves creates a dark, top-heavy mop, turning dull gold in autumn and often lit in summer by patches of gossamer webbing. The webs are the homes of tent caterpillars ("webworms"), larvae of moths who come seasonally to strip foliage from the trees when they are stressed by drought. Though often perceived as a disfiguring plague, the caterpillars pose little actual threat to the pecans and they display a curious beauty at night.

At the foot of the motts, several mounding shrubs could be added to further enclose the meadow. Shining sumac (*Rhus copallina*) and its Southwestern variant, the prairie flameleaf sumac (*R. c. v. lanceolata*), supply pale panicles of tiny midsummer blossoms that show against shiny deciduous foliage. The compound leaves turn mostly red in autumn, falling to reveal gaunt, suckering branches. These are topped by thickset lemon-scented berries and form dark winter silhouettes like gigantic sets of antlers.

The smoketree (*Cotinus obovatus*) might light the night with its upright masses of pale green, oval foliage. The veined, textural leaves have a peculiar transparency that captures light. In summer, female bushes are crowned by clouds of frothy seed. This "smoke" dances above the leaves like patches of silk and lasts through the whole of the growing season. Purple-leafed selections of the European smoketree (*Cotinus coggygria*) ordinarily bring a shadowy presence to landscapes, but they, too, show brightly at night when in flower.

Under the moon, the hop bush (*Ptelea trifoliata*) affords a dull luminescence, which it creates with chartreuse winged seeds and pale-toned flowers. On warm nights its rich green aromatic foliage adds a pungent aroma to the atmosphere, a harsh citrusy scent encouraging some to call this widespread native shrub by another name: "skunkbush." Nevertheless, the hop bush proves to be a well-mannered garden subject with a quiet elegance. In the fall its three-parted leaves turn a handsome pale yellow.

A true night-flowering prairie shrub, the sweet-scented buffalo currant (*Ribes odoratum*) might be given a place of honor towards the fore of the motts so that its long-tubed yellow blossoms could be smelled at close range. These pendant golden climes appear in small clusters at the end of spring and attract some of the first hawkmoths of the year. Although the lives of these bushes seem otherwise uneventful, their crisp-cut leaves remain handsome through summer, turning yellow in the fall. Their black berries are interesting, even though they are not especially good to eat, and the densely spreading branches afford a daytime haunt for the toads that roam the prairie at night.

Climbers

Along one end of the meadow, a low fence might support several rugged hedgerow climbers. Silver lace vine (*Polygonum aubertii*), a buckwheat from the dry steppes of western China and Tibet, is one that blooms tirelessly through heat and drought. Small white, heart-shaped flowers appear in short racemes at the tips of its wiry stems, standing out sharply before the rough masses of dark foliage. This hardy climber's perennial shoots die away in winter but spring up vigorously from the ground at the start of summer.

For sheer luminosity, the silver lace vine might be surpassed only by a few unusual clematis. The old man's beard (*Clematis drummondii*), a wild cousin of the large-flowered garden clematis, produces only modest greenish blooms and rather homely, much cut leaves. In late summer, silver puffs of feathery seeds, or achenes, swallow these rambling vines in a froth that traps the palest moonbeams. Even silkier seed heads adorn *Clematis tangutica,* a Mongolian species with golden urn-shaped flowers. More graceful backdrops for a night collection of prairie flowers could hardly be imagined.

A Few Roses

Roses are an ancient race of hardy shrubs and ramblers, most of which prefer a half-climbing existence among hedgerows and sun-drenched fields. Although metamorphosed under the hand of man, they remain prairie flowers by inclination. Fragrances of wild roses and scents of many of the older garden types recall the freshness of spring meadows; for night gardens on the prairie, any of these potent blossoms pale enough to show through the gloom are treasures.

Eglantine, or sweetbrier (*Rosa eglanteria*), might climb on the fence next to the silver lace vines so that its thorny canes have a place to sprawl. The pale pink single blossoms appear in late spring and offer a moment of interest, but the real reason to plant this prickly shrub is to enjoy its refreshingly fragrant foliage. Celebrated by Shakespeare, sweetbrier leaves emit a unique tart-apple scent, an enticing aroma that lingers after June showers and scents fingertips after only a brief rubbing.

Prairie nights might also be sweetened by the Pemberton musks, a half-hardy group of indescribably beautiful roses originated by an English clergyman early in the twentieth century. Soft saffron 'Penelope' is the most famous, gracing vigorous bushes with lax, clustered blooms. These open to yellow-centered, semidouble florets through the growing season and ripen curious greenish pink lips in autumn. Other varieties with charming names and habits—'Prosperity', 'Moonlight', 'Felicia', 'Francesca', and 'Cornelia'—offer blossoms tenderly shaded with yellow, amber, warm pink, and apricot. A few of the musks, like that beautiful witch 'Buff Beauty', have such hateful thorns that they demand placement far from any paths. It is the nature of love, how-ever, that one comes to cherish what is sometimes cursed. These flowers con-tinue to reward our eyes and noses, though their stems will make us bleed.

Where harsh winter cold threatens a few of the pale ramblers might be useful. 'New Dawn' is a creamy pink climber that yields a massed display of blossom in early spring and sputtering bloom thereafter. The apricot tinged 'Albertine', milk-toned 'Alberic Barbier', yellow-ivory 'Silver Moon', and creamy 'Gardenia' flower in April. These make sturdy vines with dark foliage to set off the flowers. The creamy *Rosa multiflora,* one of the parents of these hardy climbers, might itself be set out as a specimen where there is room. This species often reaches ten feet, producing a cascading mound dressed in April by hoards of heavy-scented blossoms.

If less space can be taken, some of the white-flowered Japanese roses like *Rosa rugosa* 'Blanc Double de Coubert' would offer sputtering soft-petaled blossoms. Large enough to show against the corrugated green foliage of the bushes, these blooms possess an unequaled sweet fragrance. Any of the older scented classes of roses, the Albas, Mosses, Damasks, Gallicas, or Noisettes, would also be welcome shrubs to mix in the prairie patch.

Although only lightly fragrant, the pale gold 'Harrison's Yellow' offers a shining vision under a spring moon and the exquisite modern shrub, 'Nevada' could hardly be approached with its snowy single blossoms. Where they are hardy, the lovely 'Mermaid' and its miniature sport, 'Happenstance', might be allowed to add their soft yellow blossoms. These bear five waxed petals sur-rounding bosses of gold stamens and appear in fleeting crops all summer.

Grasses under the Moon

More than most plants, grasses enjoy a gift of lightness. Their thin frames, eternally swaying in the breezes, capture and reflect each beam that strikes. To view a meadow in the glow of a full moon is to see a tapestry of glassy threads in patterned patches of silver, bone, ash, mud, and coal.

In conventional gardens, grasses are usually exiled from the flower bor-ders, but there is no good reason for this. The thin, mobile leaves of grasses afford natural foils for the coarser foliage of perennials. Many prairie species send out roots to penetrate the soil, improving growth for neighboring plants. The wild sod is constantly reshaping its surface as grass clumps expand and open to form miniature rings and crests. Over time a patchwork of damp hollows, dry ridges, and other small habitats comes into being, making it possible for differing plants to grow side by side. Gardeners might play upon this natural prairie diversity by devising similar small-scale niches in their borders.

Silver-blue

Four of the principle grasses of American prairies—big bluestem (*Andropogon gerardii*), little bluestem (*Schizachyrium scoparium*), switchgrass (*Panicum virgatum*), and Indiangrass (*Sorghastrum nutans*)—occur in silver or blue-gray phases as well as in common green strains. This gives them great versatility for night plantings. To surround a moonlit meadow, both the light- and dark-toned grasses might be massed in a mottled matrix.

The palest variant of big bluestem, sand bluestem (*Andropogon hallii*) is a true silver-gray. Both this variety and the more ordinary soft blue-green strains of *Andropogon* spread, in time creating rough turfs of arched, tapered foliage. These leaves hold at about a foot for most of the summer, bolting late in the year to show slender four- to six-foot stalks tipped with the three-parted purplish "turkey feet." In the fall, the leaves turn rusty before dying down to thick brown mats. Since big bluestem is slow to awaken in spring, it provides a good home for naturalized bulbs. The chalk white *Allium fraseri* and the pale lavender *Allium mobilense* are prairie onions that might make good bulb companions in the moonlight.

The shiny leaves of little bluestem arch and recurve like its large cousin, but this grass is a confirmed clumper, growing in distinctive tufts on drier upland soils. The reedy blooms rise in midsummer, reaching four feet or more. These make the plants look like stiffly upswept whisk brooms and will be either green, purplish, or silver depending on the strain of little bluestem. Autumn brings gossamer seeds and darkening foliage. In good forms, such as the cultivar 'Blaze', the leaves flare to a deep reddish-cinnamon, a coloring that lasts through half the winter.

Indiangrass exhibits coarser textures than the bluestems but is no taller. This adaptable native spreads in patches, sending up phalanxes of tapered leaves like sharp spears. Its feathery pyramids of tan-yellow blooms appear in late summer, swaying above the stiffly upright foliage. 'Sioux Blue', a selection with especially steely leaves, would be remarkable in moonlight, turning clear yellow in autumn before it ripens to a rich burnt orange.

A clump of switchgrass is often wider four feet off the ground than at the root, for this native disposes its leafy stems like a graceful arrangement set in a vase. Airy flower panicles add delicacy, despite the considerable size of the plants, which often top six feet. A fine blue selection called 'Heavy Metal' forms tight clumps three-and-one-half feet tall that turn bright yellow in autumn. Few grasses would be more arresting to view under autumn moons.

Straw

The luminous tones supplied by grasses include the browns of their drying straw. Canada wildrye (*Elymus canadensis*), a cool-season grass of American prairies, is worth planting simply for its wheatlike seed heads, which mature in early summer. As these ripen, the entire plant turns a soft brown, creating a vision of fruitfulness even through the dark of night.

Barleys (*Hordeum* spp.) provide even more feathery crops on their short stems. These winter annuals must be seeded in the fall and seem to prefer low spots where moisture stands. A nighttime patch of them in the midst of a damp meadow glows like a swirling pool of luminescent sea creatures.

In half shade or wherever the soil holds some moisture, the inland sea oats (*Chasmanthium latifolium*) might add its drooping oat-seeds to the nocturnal scene as well. These hardy clumping perennials send up leafy green shoots, resembling clusters of miniature bamboo. The showy seed heads appear above the dark green leaves in early summer, changing gradually from chartreuse to a pale, tawny brown. These last through fall, gradually falling as the plants brown and die back to short resting tufts for winter.

Dark Fountains

Although their rich greenery would be a vision of blackness, the enormous tufts of the eastern gama grass (*Tripsacum dactyloides*) would also be indispensable for the nocturnal compositions. Rising to four feet or more, this cousin of maize displays wide, slick blades that both transmit and reflect moonbeams. As one of the principal tall grasses of the American prairie, this massive plant thrives on a range of sites, taking both sun and shade. These would make ideal contrasts to the grays and browns elsewhere in the meadow.

Artemisias

With a rough framework set forth by these grasses, the meadow will be ready to be lighted by the incomparable silvers of the artemisias. These aromatic perennials were named for the goddess Artemis and may be correctly pronounced after her name, though gardeners more often utter a harsh "arte-meesia." Medicinal and culinary herbs, soft-wooded shrubs like the sagebrush of the West, and a treasure trove of silver-filigreed perennials from grasslands and seacoasts around the world all belong to *Artemisia*.

For prairie gardens the willow-leafed silver sage (*Artemisia ludoviciana*) affords the proper place to begin an exploration of this genus. Tall enough to show in the midst of the grasses or at the side of a pale-pink shrub rose, this perennial manages to be pretty yet remains untamed. Wildness is no illusion, for the running roots spread through a garden at a frightful pace. Even so, the slender plumes of frosty gray make this prairie herb among the most visually arresting of silver plants. When the clumps require weeding, as eventually will be the case, it is a pleasant task, for the aromatic leaves are the same western "sage" often sold as incense. 'Silver Queen', the best known of several cultivars, distinguishes itself with especially white, slightly cut leaves. 'Valerie Finnis', with entire foliage and a restrained habit, is even more luminous and the most desirable of the named forms. Many artemisias struggle in the heat and humidity of the South, but these are foolproof.

Another species that enjoys dampness, *Artemisia lactiflora,* is one of the few in the genus planted for its flowers. These are small and white and appear in late summer on top of the three- to five-foot stems. The leaves of this Chinese species are deep green, instead of the customary gray, so they make an effective contrast for the pale blooms. *A. lactiflora* demands a steady supply of moisture, so it might be sited in a low spot in the meadow.

Legumes

To contrast with the artemisias, the dark green prairie acacia (*Acacia hirta*) could be encouraged to grow nearby. This spreading perennial sends up wiry shoots dressed in lacy leaflets like miniature ferns. Tiny powder puffs of cream appear in late summer at the tips of the stems, which usually mature at two feet or less. Under the moon, the sprawling plants read as pools of darkness; they make terrific foils for any adjacent masses of silver or gray. As rugged as the silver sage, prairie acacia conquers any territory before it.

More restrained legumes like white prairie clover (*Petalostemon multiflorum*) might be added to the meadow for their white button flowers, while the clumped pea-blossoms of the early spring milk vetches (*Astragalus* spp.) and the loose May pyramids of white false indigo (*Baptisia alba*) provide other interpretations of the pea theme. Feathery grayed leaves distinguish the lead plant (*Amorpha canescens*), a pale pea-shrublet of sandy prairies. At night its numerous blue-purple flower spikes make the hoary bushes look like lead chandeliers covered in sinister candles of wrought metal.

Composites

The vast populations of composites, with variously rayed and rayless daisy-flowers and coarsely textural leaves, seem to have been purposefully conceived for mixing among the grasses, artemisias, and legumes of the meadow. Several pale types are worthwhile in moonlight, as most members of this family keep their flowers open at night. The disklike blossoms make an obvious show.

Truly white daisies, like the common field or ox-eye daisy (*Chrysanthemum leucanthemum*), illuminate whole meadows when they are in bloom. Their simple white-rayed, yellow-centered pinwheels possess a platinum brilliance excited by the palest moonglow. Like dandelions, these Old World wildflowers have become weeds of moist lawns and meadows. They readily naturalize in a prairie garden, keeping up with the bluestems in height.

On drier ground among short grasses like blue grama, the white flower of choice might be the native blackfoot daisy (*Melampodium leucanthemum*), a wiry perennial dotted with one-inch disks of shimmering ivory. After summer rains these little shrublets cover in blossom and several crops of flowers can be expected through the growing season in response to monsoonal flows of moisture. Although small, these little daisies paint an evening meadow with a white that outshines the stars.

More subtle effects might be wrought by planting clumps of the pale-toned *Echinacea pallida*, a slender-petaled cousin of the common purple cone flower. Drooping rays endow these sizable daisies with an ethereal grace reinforced by their gentle pink-blushed coloring. On a moonlit prairie, these ruggedly coarse perennials appear as floral ghosts, their emaciated blossoms seeming to drift and sway among the grasses. Although lacking in the spectral qualities of *E. pallida*, a rare yellow species, *Echinacea paradoxa*, would also be of value under moonlight. Like all the echinaceas, these are ideal for planting among grasses and display great resistance to drought.

Another odd prairie daisy, the rosinweed, or compass plant (*Silphium albiflorum*), lines exceptionally rough stems with large rigid leaves cut in deep lobes like a staghorn fern. These have a slightly sticky, rosinlike texture and are held in a north-south plane with the blooms, looking like chalky white sunflowers, disposed at the sides. This peculiar orientation gives these two-foot perennials a certain personality, as if the blossoms had positioned themselves to address the gardener. Poor, dry soils are their preferred home, so they might be included on one of the drier banks of the meadow.

The little dandelion blooms called Barbara's buttons (*Marshallia* spp.) belong to a few species of dwarf perennials native to the grasslands of the South. A common variety from Texas prairies, *Marshallia caespitosa*, forms large colonies, sending up scented white buttons in April and May. Other species, mostly with nondescript tufts of linear foliage, provide blooms in cream tones or pale lavenders. All make good garden flowers in moonlight.

Another Southern daisy, the Stoke's aster (*Stokesia laevis*) is known for its large cornflower-style blossoms. These are ordinarily sky blue and would be of marginal interest at night, but a rare form, the sulfur yellow 'Mary Gregory' is pale enough to be employed in nocturnal gardens. Its lax, flowering stems reach two feet, rising from compact rosettes of gray-green paddle-shaped

Pink evening primrose, *Oenothera speciosa* (Paul Cox)

Gayfeather, *Liatris mucronata*, in seed

Mock orange, *Philadelphus coronarius*

Mealy cup sage, *Salvia farinacea*, with Mexican wiregrass, *Stipa tenuissima*

leaves. Like other strains of *Stokesia*, this native perennial blooms over a long season and prefers sunny exposures with well-drained, damp soil.

The billowy mounds of *Coreopsis verticillata* 'Moonbeam' might be set before the grasses to create patches of light in the darkened meadow. Like the *Stokesia*, these pale-yellow daisies favor sandy soils, thriving especially in the middle and upper South. Their wiry green foliage provides an ideal dark backdrop for the luminous sulfur-toned petals; in winter the leaves die down to blackened masses, providing yet another experience. Not surprisingly, these hardy perennials have become great favorites in gardens, especially valued for their dense, compact growth, usually reaching eighteen to twenty-four inches.

Among the glades of switchgrass and Indiangrass, clumps of the giant coneflower (*Rudbeckia maxima*) would afford telling nocturnal accents. Both the large blossoms and the wide gray leaves would be valuable, and at seven feet in height the plants would be difficult to miss. Yellow rays surround black cones at the center of the blooms, creating a spectacle in early summer. The silver-gray leaves remain attractive year-round and make an effective contrast for grasses. Like other Southern daisies, this gigantic cousin of black-eyed Susan enjoys moist soils. More rudbeckias and tall yellow daisies such as sunflowers (*Helianthus*), ox-eye (*Heliopsis*), or sheezweed (*Helenium*) could find places in the night plantings as well. A pale-yellow giant sunflower, *Helianthus giganteus* 'Sheila's Sunshine', might be especially good.

In a differing style, the platelike flowers of white yarrow (*Achillea millefolium*) might be employed for their luminous capacities. Like ox-eye daisies, these Old World herbs have naturalized widely. Although aggressive, the fernleaf yarrow remains ideal for naturalistic plantings, reaching two to three feet in height at spring bloom. Its unblemished whiteness shows more clearly at night than the colored flowers of hybrid yarrows, and its spreading mats of foliage have no trouble competing with the toughest prairie grasses.

To close the floral year, heath asters (*Aster ericoides*) might be set through the meadow to spread their tiny white daisies, billowing like the puffs of clouds floating in the prairie sky. The dainty blooms appear along wiry stems covered in small, needlelike foliage, providing these plants with a grace that belies real toughness. After bloom, the shrublets cover in a silvery froth of ripening seed, so that at night they appear to be coated in frost.

The eastern silvery aster (*Aster concolor*) offers the more typical blue-purple flowers characteristic of this genus, but these appear on lithe wands dressed in silver foliage. One-inch, down-covered leaves gradually shrink up the four-foot stems until they reduce to scales among the flowers. This gives a silky brilliance to the plants all season.

Where the ground is permanently moist, the snowy *Boltonia asteroides* would be of value. These eastern perennials can tower up to four feet, making clouds of small white daisies in late summer. A selection from New England called 'Snowbank' is the most popular strain, but other varieties, including pale pink forms, might be tried in the South.

A close cousin of the asters, the roughleaf goldenrod (*Solidago rugosa*) is another luminous late season wildflower. This might consort with the ripening grasses in the meadow, catching the light of the autumn moons. An especially showy cultivar called 'Fireworks' provides threadlike streamers of yellow that show through the night like schools of glowing minnows. As with most goldenrods, this variety enjoys sunny positions and damp soil.

Although more often lavender, the white forms of the gayfeathers (*Liatris* spp.) can be remarkable late flowers, enduring either drought or waterlogged conditions depending on the species. Their fat wands look like exploding bomb bursts among the grasses and will ripen to silky bottle brushes of seed that last for weeks, feeding migrating birds. The dried seeds are as striking in moonlight as the flowers. *Liatris spicata* is a popular species suited to damp conditions; *L. mucronata* enjoys dry sites.

Flowers for Moonbeams

The mint family, too, contributes pale prairie flowers. Lemon-scented horsemint (*Monarda citriodora*) punctuates whorls of creamy purple blossoms with chalky or lavender bracts. The effect, like miniature tiered pagodas, gives these annuals a habit recognizable even at night. A soft lavender perennial, *Monarda fistulosa* 'Claire Grace' might also sprawl among the grasses, providing a frothy mass of tubular blossoms in midsummer.

The leaden spikes of *Salvia farinacea* 'Porcelain' in moonlight, for the calyces of the flowers have a silky luster. This near-white form of the blue mealy sage makes an easy perennial for dry positions, striking in the midst of feathery-plumed grasses. Seed company selections like 'Strata' are also pale enough for night displays, but these are not always reliably perennial.

Russian sage (*Perovskia atriplicifolia*) is endowed with branched bloom spikes of an unusual pale lavender. These join its dissected gray foliage to create an ethereal froth that makes a fantastic complement for grasses. Like the salvias, these hardy plants are among the toughest perennials.

Milkweeds (*Asclepias* spp.) have numerous forms with waxy, five-parted star blossoms in greenish-white, yellow, ivory, or pinkish tones. All are useful night flowers. Swamp milkweed (*Asclepias incarnata*), a species of damp swales, produces regal stems covered in gray-green leaves and tenderly shaded clusters of creamy lilac blooms that shine at night like frosted metal. A white-flowered selection, 'Ice Ballet' would be even more arresting, reaching four to five feet and covering in clusters of snowy stars.

A sky blue cousin of the milkweeds, the southern star (*Oxypetalum caeruleum*) warrants a place in the prairie plantings, as its fleshy flowers have a pale luster that shows through the darkness. The five-petaled blooms appear continuously at the tips of downy gray stems that often bend over with their weight. This Argentine perennial is hardy in the South, although many books suggest otherwise, usually referring to these affable flowers under the old name, 'Tweedia'.

In midspring the false gromwell (*Onosmodium occidentale*) sends up curious curling spikes of greenish-white tubular blossoms. These unfurl like the coiled tails of scorpions and give relations of the herb comfrey a peculiar grace. The lanceolate leaves have deep veins and bear stiff hairs that give the plants a slightly gray cast. False gromwell seems to do equally well in sun or shade, so it might be mixed among the prairie trees or grasses at will. The little lantern-shaped blooms emit an odd fragrance that combines jasmine with hints of chlorine.

Another flower, the downy, or prairie phlox (*Phlox pilosa*), might ramble in the night garden as well. Its light pink or lilac pinwheels sit upon narrow tubes and give these early spring blooms the aspect of true night flowers, though they are most often pollinated by bumblebees or butterflies. 'Chattahoochee' is a form with good, fragrant, pale blossoms. Since grasses are dormant when these flowers are in bloom, their stems can be encouraged to spread through the sod for a precocious display.

Later in the summer, a low spot in the meadow could sustain patches of one of the white summer phloxes (*Phlox paniculata* cvs.). There are several of these, all with tall wands of snowy blooms and good dark-green foliage. Summer phloxes thrive both in sun or partial shade, so long as moisture is unfailing. 'David' and 'Mt. Fuji' are especially fragrant varieties resistant to the mildews that afflict these popular border flowers. A related tall phlox, *Phlox carolina* 'Miss Lingard' is another good white. When well grown, these three-foot perennials will light the night more brightly than a torch.

The old-fashioned biennial called honesty, or money plant (*Lunaria annua*), might be seeded into partial shade beneath the trees. The four-petaled lavender florets are early and fragrant, but the real value of the plants comes when they ripen their satiny seedpods. These last for many weeks, catching the summer moonbeams, and are the familiar cellophane disks of dried arrangements. Their roundness is the origin of another name for this flower, moonwort, which the botanical title references as well. *Lunaria* comes in a white strain ('Alba') and in a variegated form, both of nocturnal interest. The hardy plants usually die after flowering but may be kept coming along by setting out fresh seed in the fall.

The glaucous holly leaves of prickly poppy (*Argemone albiflora*) embroider with milky veins that show at night even when the handsome blooms, like rumpled white handkerchiefs, are not on display. When the snowy flowers appear in early summer, they stand out like freshly bleached linen. Abundant prickles make this tough perennial unpleasant to encounter at close range, but one could hardly imagine a garden citizen more striking in moonlight.

The annual opium poppies (*Papaver somniferum*) might also be included in the meadow for their rosettes of silky, glaucous foliage. Cabbagey flowers appear in spring and come mostly in pastel shades of pink, maroon, or lavender, so a patch of these old-fashioned blooms assumes a charming maudlin appearance under the moon. These are easy garden flowers, thriving on the poorest soils when seeded in early fall.

Poppy mallows, or wine cups (*Callirhoe* spp.), known mostly in dark purple, also occur in white and in starry pale lavender strains that show well at night. These cousins of hollyhocks are among the most enduring prairie flowers, often growing from a tuberous root. Their slender stems and finely cut leaves, either upright or trailing, are beautifully foiled by grassy companions.

Some of the penstemons, like the light lavender forms of wild foxglove (*Penstemon cobaea*), would be arresting to set in patches through the prairie. Like fat, inflated snapdragons, these spikes of muddied white reach up to two feet, flowering in mid April. The leathery-leafed plants do well on thin, dry soils. Later blooming *P. digitalis* might also be viewed pleasantly in moonlight. Its branched wands of tubular near white blossoms thrust from lush basal rosettes in early summer. In the Nebraska strain, 'Husker's Red', the tongue-shaped leaves suffuse in vinous tints, magnifying the value of the blooms.

Small blossoms, like the pale primrose *Patrinia scabiosifolia*, will also glow through the prairie dark, for their tender yellow has an unusually luminous quality. The tiny unscented flowers appear clustered above much-cut leaves that look like bunches of celery. A cousin of valerian native to Japan, *Patrinia* thrives on moist soils and seems to do well among other prairie flowers. Although not so glowing as these, the yellow foxglove (*Digitalis ambigua*) and the primrose hollyhock (*Alcea rugosa*) are other blooms that would be tall and striking enough to include among the meadow flowers.

Peonies (*Paeonia lacteus*) have a long history in prairie gardens and may often be found persisting about old homesteads. These huge fragrant blooms sit among mounds of dark, lustrous foliage, giving the plants a commanding presence. As natives of northern China, peonies generally sulk in the heat of the southern states, but at least one, the old double white 'Festiva Maxima', can be counted on to flower early and reliably. These enormous blooms fill with white cabbagey petals and handfuls of slender red filaments that arrange themselves irregularly towards the center. At night, the sweet-scented globes seem to be streaked with dark bolts of lightning. Yellowing fall foliage provides another evening show later in the season.

The lightly branched stems of snow-on-the-mountain (*Euphorbia bicolor*) offer one of the most certain sources of white in the prairie. Simple gray-green leaves line the two- to three-foot stalks, becoming ivory-edged bracts at the tips of the stems. The effect is like small green and white poinsettias, which makes sense, since these annual spurges are relations of that tropical Mexican flower. Snow-on-the-mountain also ranks among the most drought-tolerant blooms and will reseed happily on dry, thin soils. In late summer, its milky wands can be seen shining across the garden at a considerable distance.

True Night Flowers

Although any pale leaves or flowers in the meadow might draw human eyes at night, the attentions of moths remains firmly fixed on those perfumed blossoms of strictly nocturnal habit. One of the most obvious of these, the blazing star (*Mentzelia* spp.) opens its exotic-looking flowers at dusk. The common strain, *Mentzelia lindleyi*, is a wildflower from the grasslands of the far West. The golden blossoms, with five satiny petals surrounding brushes of yellow stamens, recall St. John's wort, but they have a sweet fragrance unknown to that flower. These annuals grow readily from fall sown seed.

A perennial blazing star native to the great plains, *Mentzelia decapetala* is an even better subject for prairie plantings, with three- to four-inch, ten-petaled blooms like creamy cactus blossoms. These large, silky pinwheels open in late afternoon at the tips of rough, ungainly stems, closing early the next morning. At night they have a magical beauty. As might be expected, they also have a pleasant fragrance to attract the hawkmoths. Sparse, sandpapery leaves cover the stems of these otherwise charming perennials and will stick to clothing like Velcro, prompting another common name: stick leaf. *M. decapetala* grows easily in any sunny, well-drained position.

Blue stars (*Amsonia* spp.) are hardy representatives of the periwinkle family (*Apocynaceae*), many of whose members tend towards nocturnal habits. Several of these feathery perennials thrive in prairies, providing clusters of scented blooms in early summer. These resemble phloxes and usually come in a shade of blue so pale as to be visible at night. *Amsonia tabernaemontana* is the common blue star of the east, with compact clusters of narrow-leafed stems and a preference for moist soils; *A. hubrectii* prefers dry shade and makes tufts of slender leaves topped in spring with steel blue flowers; *A. ciliata* has more questing roots and ranges through the southern prairies from Texas to the Carolinas. All are fragrant and their brightly yellowing fall foliage provides another treat late in the season.

One of the scourges of sandy prairies in the South, the bull nettle (*Cnidoscolus texanus*) is also one of the most delectable night flowers of summer. In the midst of its rough-cut leaves, covered in threatening prickles, rise clusters of five-lobed blossoms that seem to be made of white velvet. These look and smell like an exotic jasmine, and they ripen to three-valved pods filled with tasty nutlike seeds. Although easy growing, these plants can inflict a painful sting. Their deep taproots are difficult to eradicate, so they should only be invited to the garden if they can be positioned away from traffic.

A more genteel flower, the prairie lily (*Zephyranthes drummondii*) might be planted freely through the meadow. The white funnels of this little amaryllis from the Texas prairies appear after summer rains, opening at dusk to scent the air with a heavy perfume. Strappy gray leaves emerge from the tops of its globular, brown-skinned bulbs. This pale foliage grows through the winter and might be a nocturnal attraction in itself. The real magic of these plants can only be felt when a whole meadow of their waxy white goblets opens simultaneously on an early summer evening, calling the hawkmoths to come and sip sweet nectar.

On a more grand scale the lemony blooms of certain night-fragrant *Hemerocallis* might be added for their glowing trumpets. Only a few of the species in this popular genus are truly nocturnal, but these are flowers of special beauty. The botanical name, *Hemerocallis*, which means "beautiful for a day," inspires the common name, "daylily," and refers to the peculiar habits of these hardy perennials, whose blossoms usually last only twenty-four hours.

The night-flowering types, originating from the meadows of China, open their slender yellow flowers as dusk falls, keeping them through the next morning. Although the original species, *Hemerocallis citrina* and *H. altissima*, are not themselves common in gardens, a whole host of their hybrids, mostly in varying shades of yellow, may be had. These often inherit evening blooming tendencies and the delicious custard fragrance of their wild ancestors. Like other daylilies, the night-blooming forms are flowers of early summer. They are among the most foolproof perennials.

A garden plant sometimes grown as *H. citrina* is, in fact, one of its early hybrids, an old variety called 'Baroni'. Its broad, dark leaves have silvery undersides and make grassy clumps that turn a pretty yellow in the fall. The slender flowers expand stiff citron segments in early evening, releasing a sweet fragrance. Since the blooms are held aloft on three-foot stems, they mix happily with stands of little bluestem or other medium tall grasses.

The old standby 'Hyperion' provides another yellow sturdy enough for naturalistic treatment. Gracefully curving petals give the slender flowers an orchidlike beauty. In the moonlight, they can be appreciated at great distance, for their light lemony tone and aristocratic bearing have no trouble showing through the gloom. The splendid fragrance is an added bonus.

Innumerable other yellow daylilies might be added to the meadow, especially forms with small or spidery blooms, for these would be most in keeping with the blurry aesthetics of the night. The old-fashioned lemon lily (*Hemerocallis flava*), the tiny spray-flowering *H. multiflora*, and the dwarf yellow tetraploid hybrid 'Bitsy' might be mentioned in particular for their general hardiness. A delicate yellow novelty, 'Move Over Moon' could be set in the meadow to gather for late suppers, as its huge chalice-shaped blossoms bear succulent, delectably edible petals with a sweet, lemony flavor.

Queens of the Prairie

Above all of these, however, the four-fold funnels of the evening primrose reign supreme. This varied race is dear to the heart of every prairie dweller, for these soft-textured flowers redeem the vacant fields, roadsides, and waste places that otherwise fill daily scenery with indifference. Evening primroses (*Oenothera* spp.) seem to have been particularly equipped for this role and are at their best on the poorest, driest soils. Over eighty species may be had from the fields and plains of the Americas.

Two yellow varieties, the Missouri primrose (*Oenothera macrocarpa*) and the river primrose (*O. hookeri*), have already received mention for their value as border flowers. Both would be worthy of inclusion in the prairie plantings, where their sprawling and upright stems, respectively, might mingle among the grasses. The huge lemon funnels of these species would be visible at night from far across the meadow, and on most evenings of the summer, a steady whirring from the wings of the hawkmoths' might be perceived around them from several feet away.

The most delicious of this huge tribe in fragrance, and one of the most lovely flowers in the genus, belongs to the white-tufted primrose (*Oenothera caespitosa*). A native of the Rocky Mountain states, this species grows in short rosettes comprised of narrow, sinuate leaves. These gray-green tufts sit down among the prairie grasses where the plants flower over many weeks of summer.

As evening draws close, the coarse green buds begin to split, revealing the silky corollas of the four-inch wide flowers. These slowly swell, so that the leathery sepals enfolding the blooms suddenly break, allowing the clear white funnels to expand. When fully open the four heart-shaped petals create a distinctive outline like a rounded Maltese cross. A powerful lemon-magnolia fragrance radiates a message of allure from the green-tinged throats of the blossoms, adding a heady perfume to their considerable beauty. As morning arrives, the spent flowers blush rose before folding limply away.

Although short lived, *O. caespitosa* grows rapidly from seeds and will usually self-sow on gravelly or gritty soils. These plants are native to high elevations, so they should be given some shading in warm climates. A similar-looking primrose with running roots, *Oenothera pallida* is sometime offered as a summer annual. These might be happily mixed among the shorter grasses at the edge of the meadow.

Although nearly devoid of fragrance, the pale blooms of the showy Mexican primrose (*Oenothera berlandieri*) have the capacity to smother their native prairies, painting color over the earth on a grand scale. During early spring, sheets of their rosy petals give a warm glow to meadows. The rambling stems of this rambunctious perennial thread their way among grasses so that every inch is covered in bloom. Since they make foliage mostly in winter, the showy primroses make good companions for summer grasses. Their April flowers usually finish by the time other prairie perennials begin growth.

Under irrigation and in cool climates, this Southwestern flower sometimes extends its period of bloom. There is even a named form, 'Siskiyou', selected for continuous flowering. In warm regions, however, it finishes growth in late spring like other forms of the species. Although the spreading roots may be difficult to restrain and the plants might look bedraggled when past their peak, the pink chiffon flowers of the showy primrose give great charm in their season. Since the blooms are borne low to the ground, they provide a true floral carpet. At night the fields seem to be radiating the warmth from the earth itself.

One curious aspect of these blooms is that the pale ones are usually the largest, while the deepest rose flowers are smaller than average. It is as if each blossom had been allotted its measure of rosy paint and the intensity of the hue was dependent on the size of the canvas. In nature something not too different from this must actually be taking place. The width of these blooms may depend on the dimensions of individual cells in their petals, which, in turn, may be endowed separately with pigments.

To finish these plantings, a graceful cousin of the oenotheras, the False-gaura (*Stenosiphon linifolius*), might be set among the tallest grasses to light the night with its silvery candles. Although the white flowers of this tall, wire-stemmed perennial seem tiny in comparison to the ravishing evening primroses, they carry themselves so lightly atop the stems that any slight breeze causes a stir. Like the grasses that define this vast territory, they wave with the incessant winds. Under the light of the prairie moon they seem to beckon. Come closer. Look. Smell. Listen. Perceive what is really here.

There, where the darts are dyed,
where the shields are painted,
are the perfumed white flowers;
flowers of the heart,
the flowers of the Giver of Life
open their blossoms.
Their perfume is sought by the lords.

FIVE

The Tropic Moon

here is a richness to the life of warm climates that eclipses the restrained editions of nature found in temperate realms. The bold vegetation hangs with the tepid dew of the evenings, exploding through the heavy atmosphere in unbridled diversity. Prattling birds and amphibians chirp from among the shadows while a steady murmuring of unseen insects hints at innumerable beings lurking among leaves and branches. Through this abundance, the omnipresent scents of growth and decay combine with the sweet aromas of floral nectaries to express the fullness and potency of tropic nature.

Heat dominates daylight hours in tropical latitudes, so more than anywhere else, these warmer climes are places where the life of night assumes first importance. The bleaching rays of the sun can be trying to flowers and to the creatures that pollinate them. In contrast, the lingering warmth and humidity of evening provides an ideal accompaniment for the alluring fragrances of the night blooms and their consorts.

In the southern United States, the warm summer season affords a near tropical environment suited to many night flowers. A nocturnal garden is not practical but essential here, for the life of summer carries on mostly in darkness. Many fabulous subtropical flowers belong among the true night bloomers. Their pale forms and sweet, penetrating fragrances can shape the entire experience of gardens in the South.

Jasmines

The most famous night-scented flowers, the jasmines (*Jasminum* spp.), come from a varied race of half-climbing shrubs and clambering vines and belong to the same family as the sweet olive. Many of the hardier species have yellow flowers that are nearly scentless, but the tender white jasmines supply treasured essences for perfumes and for flavoring teas and other foods. The process of *effleurage*, in which blossoms are pressed between shallow layers of fat so that their scents can be absorbed and later distilled into alcohol, is still used to prepare fragrances from these waxy petaled flowers of delight.

The variety favored for this industry and the original jasmine of literature, *Jasminum officinale*, is the poet's jasmine. As is typical for many subtropical varieties in the genus, the species bears four- or five-lobed blooms united into a short tube. These fragrant white stars present in clusters along leafy clambering stems, appearing for several weeks of the summer. Reportedly, the poet's jasmine is a food plant for hawkmoths, not only the nectar sipping adults but also their larvae, which feed on this plant's foliage. Everything about the poet's jasmine seems to reveal an underlying nocturnal rhythm.

The original home of *Jasminum officinale* remains lost in the mists of distant history, but a robust strain called *affine*, or "grandiflorum," still grows wild in the Himalayan foothills. These half-hardy vines may have come into gardens from the subtropical scrub forest of North India or around the Black Sea. Poet's jasmine was known as *jasemin* to the ancient Persians. The Arabic *ysmin*, Chinese *Yeh-hsi-ming*, and anglicized "gethsamyne," "jessamine," "gelsemine," and "jessimy" all seem to derive from this old original name.

In American gardens, the true poet's jasmine remains relatively rare, save in California, where the lax, rambling stems of this species bear flowers over a long season, basking in the cool fogs of the Pacific. The intemperate heat of the Southeast fosters only brief bloom from this species, which seems to grow too lavishly, making leaves at the expense of flowers and succumbing to freezes when severe weather threatens.

Although tender, the Arabian jasmine (*Jasminum sambac*) makes a better garden flower for the humid South. It seems to revel in the heat of summer, growing and flowering lustily in the dog days of August. Like the poet's jasmine, this species has such a long history in gardens that its origins are suspect; a guess would be that it derives from somewhere on the Indian subcontinent. The superlative fragrance of the Arabian jasmine, alive with the aromas of orange-blossom and gardenia, is even more legendary than the heady scent of the poet's jasmine.

The most floriferous form of the species travels under the name 'Maid of Orleans'. This single-flowered strain makes a tidy bush covered with wrinkled, ovate leaves, continuously gathered with small clusters of blunt-petaled creamy blossoms. The plant reaches only a few feet in height and sharp frosts will cut the spreading stems to the ground, but along the Gulf, these vigorous plants recover and prove drought tolerant when established. One small bush of this variety is enough to scent a garden for yards around. In India, where the Arabian jasmine is especially revered, its Hindu name translates as "moonlight of the grove."

A double form of the species called 'Grand Duke of Tuscany' appears in some collections. The cultivar name commemorates an actual duke who, in the 1600s, hoarded these plants in his garden, not permitting cuttings or layers to be taken. This double strain makes a better container subject than garden flower, for the upright stems develop as an odd, weak-growing column rather than as a good shrub. Fragrant, fully double blossoms, like tiny ivory camellias, appear sparingly at the ends of the stems.

A really exotic species planted in the warmest parts of the South, the angel-wing jasmine (*Jasminum nitidum*) makes a more practical addition for garden beds. Its sprawling mounds of glossy green, narrow-pointed leaves reach three to four feet. The milky one-inch blooms are formed of slender lobes that give a spidery look to the flowers, and they send forth a delicious perfume that carries far on the evening air. Although native to the entirely tropical Admiralty Islands, established angel-wing jasmines usually recover from frost and may be planted safely along the Gulf Coast. Farther north, these ever-blooming shrubs make fine plants for pots on summer patios.

J. multiflorum displays more of a climbing nature than the angel-wing jasmine, but bears similar, lightly fragrant blooms. This tender Indian species is common in Florida, where its starry eight- to ten-petaled blossoms appear through the summer among lush, velvety foliage. Spanish jasmine (*J. grandiflorum*) and Madeira jasmine (*J. odoratissimum*) are other tender climbers that provide better fragrance; both are valued in perfumery. Like the poet's jasmine, these vines bloom for a short season in the heat of the South, but are still of some value in sections where they will not freeze annually.

Another climber, the South African *J. tortuosum*, is hardier and also splendidly fragrant. This species makes an enchanting vine for arbors or garden rooms where the glossy leaves will not stand undue exposure to hard freezing weather. The deep-green foliage is an asset and helps make the most of the waxy five-lobed blossoms. For practical purposes, this variety is the best substitute for true poet's jasmine in the humidity and warmth of the South.

Rosy jasmine (*J. polyanthum*) is another half-hardy climber, cherished for its multitudes of rose-tinged blossoms. If not damaged by temperatures below fifteen degrees, the little pink buds open in late winter, exposing white tubular blooms that smother these vines for a week or two. These luxuriant

Fragrant gladiolus or acidanthera,
Gladiolus callianthus

Right: A Mexican spider lily, *Hymenocallis maximiliani*, opening its flowers at dusk

White angel's trumpet, *Brugmansia* × *candida*
(Greg Grant)

Single tuberose, *Polianthes tuberosa*
'Mexican Single'

Variegated giant cane,
Arundo donax 'Variegata'

flowers send a pleasant, musky-sweet aroma onto the cool spring air. In the South, flowering ends with the advent of warm weather, although in mild California gardens they are nearly ever-blooming.

What is probably the hardiest of the fragrant jasmines is a yellow-flowered species long grown under the name Italian jasmine. Correctly, this is a vining clone of the shrubby jasmine (*Jasminum humile*) called 'Revolutum'. Although not so hardy as the ordinary bush form of the species, Italian jasmine succeeds in the coastal South, at least, where it makes a long arching climber festooned with velvety buds of sulfur yellow. These expand to warmly fragrant stars from spring through autumn. This old garden form was introduced to Italian gardens in the mid nineteenth century but seems to originate in nature from the Himalayan region.

Pinwheels

The ordinary garden jasmine of the South actually has only a distant relation to the these true jasmines. Instead, the so-called star, or confederate jasmine (*Trachelospermum jasminoides*), turns out to be a fragrant representative of the periwinkle family (*Apocynaceae*). Although its white, five-petaled star blossoms casually resemble *Jasminum* flowers, they exhibit a tell-tale pinwheel orientation that marks them as members of yet another clan of night bloomers.

Such botanical details mean little to gardeners, who cherish these fragrant vines for the same reasons they love the true jasmines. Likewise, the night moths are just as fond of the impostors. Who could not surrender his heart to a sweet bower smothered each May in little clusters of drooping stars and leathery leaves glossed like pieces of jade enamel?

In the lower South, this evergreen "jasmine" is the customary vine for training up walls in private courtyards, where the leafy stems often make a charming tracery against old bricks. These climbers grow rapidly enough to make good cover on wire mesh or chain-link fences and may even be used as ground cover on sunny banks or under thirsty-rooted trees like live oaks. Temperatures below fifteen degrees F damage the leaves and stems, but on the whole, these natives of south central China give good performance. Wherever they are planted, their sweet fragrance seeps through the evening air, mixing with the night breezes in exquisite delicacy.

There is a variegated strain of confederate jasmine that might be of use in night gardens, although it seems to be more frost sensitive than the common types. Its cream-marbled leaves show nicely against dark masonry or wide tree trunks, and the pale vines might be trained on frames as fragrant subjects for pots on a summer terrace.

A primrose yellow *Trachelospermum* sometimes called "mandaianum" is a more vigorous garden plant with better cold tolerance. The especially nice flowers bear triangular petals that are wider than ordinary white confederate jasmines, making a fine show in early May. Although listed as a form of *T. jasminoides*, this yellow-bloomer might actually be a flowering variant of the Asian jasmine (*Trachelospermum asiaticum*) that otherwise rarely blooms in the garden strains planted for ground cover.

Along the Gulf Coast and in Florida, dark mounds of Natal plums (*Carissa macrocarpa*) carry white pinwheel blooms that look like large versions of *Trachelospermum* flowers and smell even more delicious. Like many plants in the periwinkle family, these African shrubs bleed a milky sap when pricked. Natal plums are especially popular in seaside plantings; their leathery green foliage endures salt spray and looks handsome against the expansiveness of a sandy beach. Fat purplish red fruits follow the ivory blooms and taste something like sweet cranberries when ripe. Since the bushes are ever-blooming, fruits in various stages of development appear together with the scented flowers, making a festive display all year.

Ordinary strains of Natal plum develop sharp, branched spines at the ends of the twigs, but certain dwarf selections like 'Boxwood Beauty' may be had without this formidable armature. Varieties like 'Prostrata' or 'Tuttle' have spreading habits that make them useful as ground cover; 'Fancy' is a tall type suited for hedging in regions where annual frost is unlikely. Like the tender jasmines, these deep-rooted shrubs recover from occasional freezes that blacken top growth, but they cannot really be planted where frost is a regular visitor. They are certainly beautiful and fragrant enough to warrant pots on a summer patio in colder regions.

Indian carnation, or crape jasmine (*Tabernaemontana divaricata*), provides another favorite subtropical bloom, best known in a double form called 'Flore Pleno'. Lustrous green leaves and creamy swirled blossoms combine to create plants vaguely reminiscent of gardenias. On close inspection, *Tabernaemontana* reveals bifurcating stems and creamy sap that mark it as another nocturnal cousin of the periwinkle. Like *Carissa*, these suckering shrubs need shelter from frequent frost but otherwise grow easily, enduring heat and drought. The ivory pinwheel blooms have a pleasant fragrance that becomes stronger at night. Another sweet-scented species, *Tabernaemontana holstii* displays small clusters of single white, yellow-centered pinwheels among its baylike leaves.

Other subtropical blossoms of this family have become popular for bedding in the southern states. A half-climbing shrub, the golden *Allamanda cathartica*, and a rosy-pink twining vine, *Mandevilla* 'Alice DuPont', are both well known as summer flowers for mailbox posts. Both are lightly fragrant and visible at night. They grow rampantly in warm weather but are best sheltered from hard frost. A white Mandevilla called Chilean jasmine (Mandevilla laxa) has a powerful gardenia fragrance; certain strains of Allamanda like the old cultivar 'Nobilis' emit a strong scent of magnolia.

The most obvious shrubs of the periwinkle tribe in Gulf Coast gardens remain the oleanders (Nerium oleander), most of which are day bloomers with big trusses of unscented pink, red, or white blossoms. The common white sorts are worth including in nocturnal landscapes for their arresting combination of dark foliage and immaculate bloom, but some lesser known oleanders are even better suited to evening plantings. Certain types with fragrant flowers, descendants of the Indian Nerium odorum, seem to be slightly evolved to attract nocturnal pollinators, for they produce a pleasant, musky-vanilla aroma that is strongest at night and early morning. Although many scented oleander forms are tender, at least one cultivar, an old saffron yellow called 'Mathilde Ferrier', seems hardy through the garden range of the species. This antique French clone displays clusters of "hose-in-hose" style double blossoms over a long season. It makes a superb addition to a collection of subtropical night flowers. Like most oleanders, it roots readily from stem cuttings inserted directly in soil or in cups of water.

The most deliciously fragrant of the nocturnal pinwheel-blossoms belongs to the Plumeria, or frangipani, a succulent cousin of the oleanders from tropical America. Supposedly, these sparsely branched shrubs were discovered by the botanist Frangipani when he set foot at Antigua with Columbus. Plumeria have since become popular dooryard plants, for they grow readily from cuttings, bearing their large clusters of sweet-scented blooms through the whole of summer. The common Mexican species, Plumeria acuta, drops its pointed leaves in the winter, leaving the thick, milky-sapped stems starkly bare. These shrubs require shelter from hard frost but need little else during their winter dormancy. They are perfectly happy left dry in pots, nestled in some corner of a cluttered garage.

With the return of warm weather, magnolialike leaves and clustered flowers emerge swiftly from the apex of the Plumeria branches, making tufts at the tips like the crowns of a strangely floriferous palm. For best bloom, these plants should be repotted and fertilized each spring, taking care not to damage the ends of the stems that bear the flowers for the season. Several attractive color forms of Plumeria may be found in warm shades of apricot, red, and pink, but the best scented sorts are usually the common white and yellow strains. These have aromas so delicious that they compel attention.

An evergreen species sometimes grown in South Florida, Plumeria obtusa demands more care and should be wintered in a greenhouse, if possible. Its clustered snowy flowers, born against glossy, oblong leaves, are worth the effort, for they smell even more wonderfully than the common frangipani.

'White Singapore' is the most popular strain, and there is a handsome dwarf ideal for large pots on a subtropical patio. It was this species that provided the "delicious flowery fragrance" smelled by Columbus's sailors as they approached the islands of the West Indies, where this plant is a native.

Cape Jasmines

Early May in the South is a time when warm Gulf winds sweep inland, breathing sensuality into the evening. In gardens, the silvered moon casts light on alabaster blossoms, sizable flowers whose overt eroticism enthralls the nose before they can be spotted in the darkness. These belong to the most wanton of scented garden shrubs, the cape jasmine (*Gardenia jasminoides*).

The superb flowers have a vague pinwheel form that seems to place them with the periwinkles, but glossy green leaves held in whorls of three mark these emblems of desire as cousins of coffee and *Ixora* instead. Half-hardy natives of China, the lustrous leafed gardenias have held favored positions in gardens since the they were introduced. Their overpowering scent, like an enriched compote of jasmine and tuberose, has sunk into the collective memory of generations.

Several of the garden forms of *Gardenia* can only be counted hardy near the Gulf, while other variants perform north to Virginia. Cultivars such as the popular 'Veitchii' were selected decades ago for their ability to bloom in greenhouses over the winter months; although beautiful in pots, these make poor garden plants north of Florida, since they flower only when days are short. Standard gardenias such as 'Mystery', 'Candle Light', and 'First Love' provide bushy plants with lustrous foliage and double flowers in early summer; 'August Beauty' makes an upright shrub with slender leaves and many medium-sized blooms from May until frost. Dwarf gardenias like the prostrate 'Radicans' and its cream-splashed sport 'Radicans Variegata' make attractive edging plants with a scattering of semidouble blooms over the summer. These popular cultivars are generally hardy through the middle South. Unlike most acid lovers, cape jasmines enjoy direct sun and will tolerate exposed positions if provided with rich soil and plenty of summer moisture. Where soils are alkaline, the potential reward of their fragrant, waxy white blooms justifies excavating and preparing the special acid beds they require.

Single forms usually called "star gardenias" are less popular than the opulent double cultivars but are no less fragrant or deserving of garden space. 'Kleins Hardy', a single-flowered form valuable for cold-hardiness, is the most reliable gardenia where temperatures regularly drop into the low teens. Along the Gulf Coast another single gardenia, *Gardenia thunbergia*, makes a large, angularly branched shrub. This fragrant African species is not especially cold

Queen of the night, *Selenicereus grandiflorus*

A night-blooming cereus, *Harrisia bonplandii*

Hardy night-blooming cereus, *Selenicereus spinulosus*

Confederate jasmine, *Trachelospermum jasminoides* (Greg Grant)

Fragrant crinum lily, *Crinum* x 'Alamo Village'

hardy, but it seems to endure adverse soil conditions. Where heavy clays or calcareous earths are common in Florida and Texas, this species provides understocks for grafting standard gardenias.

Citrus

As days shorten, the fall air fills with an ambrosial fragrance that seems to pervade all of nature. The droning of bees may be followed to the source of the aroma: waxy white star blossoms of citrus. In the tea factories of China, the thick petaled orange blossoms have long been used as a flavoring, just as blossoms of Arabian jasmine are mixed into the teas of India. Like bay-laurels bearing innumerable sweet jasmine-flowers, citrus provide a remarkable measure of fragrance for gardens. Although the lustrous leaves recede to blackness at night, the ripening yellow-orange fruits hang like celestial spheres in the moonlight as the sweet scents of the clustered, five-petaled blooms reach outwards into the darkness.

Along the Gulf, hardy citrus like satsumas, kumquats, calamondins, and 'Meyer' lemons may be planted in protected courtyards or other sheltered garden spaces. These make ornamental trees or shrubs with flowers at odd seasons from fall through midsummer. Fragrant citrus suited to container culture or gardens in frost-free areas include grapefruit, oranges, and citrons. A novelty, the 'Ponderosa' lemon produces oversized yellow fruits with thick, aromatic rinds. This tender hybrid of lemon and citron has especially large fragrant blooms. There is also a variegated form of 'Ponderosa', striking for a tub on a moonlit patio.

Hardy, or trifoliate, orange (*Poncirus trifoliata*) might be planted safely though all of the southern states and will make a show of its white flowers in April. Unfortunately, and in spite of the usually glowing comments found in the garden literature, only rare forms of this thorny, deciduous citrus ally have any significant fragrance. A better choice for scent, the evergreen mock orange (*Pittosporum tobira*) provides an invaluable foundation shrub hardy through the middle South, perfuming the spring air nearly as well as true citrus. The fine variegations of this species, available in both standard (three to four feet) and dwarf (one to two feet) selections, are ideal for nocturnal displays, making elegant mounds of rosetted foliage.

Port Wine

Mixed in luxuriant bosques with these fragrant evergreens, the fruity scented port wine magnolia, or banana shrub (*Michelia figo*), might fill summer evenings with tropic mystery. A dwarf cousin of the magnolia, the banana

shrub has long been a favorite in Gulf Coast gardens. Its pale auburn lilylike
blooms seem to open only halfway and are tucked shyly among its waxy leaves
so that they are difficult to view even in daytime. Yet, at night their ripe
banana-wine scent disperses widely over the humid air.

On good soils these densely rounded Asiatic shrubs reach ten feet. They
withstand cold through the lower South, at least, and are fairly easy growing.
One hybrid, *Michelia* x *foggii*, has bigger, magnolia-style leaves and grows with
a strong upright habit, eventually making a small tree. Waxen white fragrant
blooms resembling saucer magnolias hang among its evergreen branches in
the spring.

Also fruit scented, the sweet bubby bush, or Carolina allspice
(*Calycanthus floridus*), adds an exotic flare to damp woodlands. This popular
ally of the wintersweet produces its scented brownish red star blossoms in summer among textured aromatic leaves, shedding in winter to rest as a bare mass
of twigs. This native shrub can add fragrance to moonlit plantings, but
Sinocalycanthus sinensis, a rare Chinese cousin of the Carolina allspice, might
be more appropriate, since its larger glossier leaves frame starry white blossoms.

Nightshades

How mysteriously beautiful the flowers of the evening can be is revealed further by several of the nightshades. This mostly tropical family includes some
of the most flamboyant nocturnal blooms. *Nicotiana*, *Petunia*, and *Datura
inoxia* have already been mentioned as hardy border flowers, but in the subtropics, the most magnificent member of the family *Solanaceae* must be the
angel's trumpet, *Brugmansia*.

Like many nightshades, these weedy-looking, poisonous herbs grow
wild in Latin America, where they reach treelike proportions among the
tropic hills. Eight-inch blooms, called *floripondio* in their homelands, appear
among equally large leaves in winter or all year at higher elevations. Like
gigantic pendant funnels, these blossoms suspend from mostly horizontal
branches abundantly furnished with coarse, vaguely lobed foliage.

The most fragrant angel's trumpet, *Brugmansia* x *candida*, purportedly
originated as a hybrid of two Ecuadorian species. Under the moon, its slender milk-white trumpets, either single or double, droop from the rough-
leafed branches like ghostly apparitions. Another species, *B. versicolor*, has
blooms that flare out like ivory evening gowns, and these often fade to peach
as they age. Warm colors also show up in garden hybrids, like the glowing
salmon 'Charles Grimaldi', sulfury 'Jamaican Yellow', and light raspberry
'Ecuador Pink'. All are scented with the heady sweet night fragrance preferred by hawkmoths.

The pulpy stalks of *Brugmansia* collapse with hard frost, but established plants regrow rapidly when warm weather returns. Rich, moist soil is their only requirement, and the vigorous plants usually exceed six feet by summer's end, suckering to form broad clumps over time. Along the Gulf, flowering begins late in the year and continues until frost. In the upper South, short days promote earlier blooming and the angel's trumpets may be used as summer perennials, so long as their crowns are protected over winter with a good mulch.

In many other areas, summer days are too long and autumn passes too rapidly to winter for these wonders, unless they are protected in greenhouses. In consolation, the Indian *Datura metel* offers blooms nearly as large and equally fragrant. The standard garden form has double purple flowers, but a creamy yellow may be had and would be a choice addition to a moonlit collection of tropical flowers. These convoluted amber funnels smell deliciously of vanilla and ripen to prickly capsules, called "thorn apples," which provide abundant seed. Hardy through most of the South, on rich soil *Datura metel* grows rapidly enough to be treated as a summer annual.

The experience of a garden often turns on fleeting moments, so a plant whose exuberance transcends time is to be specially cherished. Another tropical American nightshade, *Brunfelsia pauciflora,* has earned the charming epithet "yesterday-today-and-tomorrow" for its amazing habits. Each April these pleasantly leafy shrubs disappear in masses of flared, tubular blooms that first open rich purple, fade to light lavender on their second day, and thence to leaden white on their third, all the while smelling richly of gardenias.

'Floribunda' is the common cultivar seen in partly shaded Gulf Coast gardens, and one could hardly ask for a more endearing and undemanding dwarf shrub. Although deciduous in hard frost, these soft-stemmed plants seem remarkably hardy when established and grow well in any ordinary garden soil. For near frost-free positions or containers, an even more exotic cousin, the "lady of the night" (*Brunfelsia americana*), might be added to moonlit compositions so its long-tubed ivory blooms could scent the air in summer.

Another magnificent plant for a frostless conservatory or garden room, the cup of gold (*Solandra maxima*) grows as a massive vine. With six-inch oval leaves along its rampant stems the gigantic eight-inch blooms seem in perfect proportion. These come in late winter and are shaped like deep urns colored golden yellow and gently striped with purple-brown. The vines grow best during cool parts of the year, sulking in summer heat, but are otherwise easy so long as they are protected from frost. The luminous flowers are big enough to rival the moon.

Of all the tropic nightshades, however, the most potent at night is the least visible. The Fragrance of the Night (*huele de noche*), or West Indian night jessamine (*Cestrum nocturnum*), asserts its presence under the moon not with dramatic form but with a narcotically sweet fragrance emitted by its flowers only at night. This scent is so overpowering that for some persons it is the cause of illness. For most gardeners, however, it is the *sine qua non* of the subtropic summer evening; nothing is sweeter.

Although they have a certain eerie, unearthly quality, the yellow-green tubular flowers of the night jessamine possess little real ornament. The plants themselves are ordinary-looking shrubs with lax stems covered in simple pointed leaves. Willow leafed jasmine (*Cestrum parqui*), a Chilean species nearly identical to C. *nocturnum*, has more slender foliage and less resistance to cold. Other *Cestrum* display noticeably colored blooms, including yellow-orange and ivory shades that might show up in night gardens, but these species lack the celebrated fragrances of their nocturnal kin. All the *Cestrum* seem to be damaged by hard frost, but most, including the night jessamine, may be grown as perennials in the lower South. Set near a doorway or in a secluded courtyard, their mysterious fragrance transports passersby into other worlds.

Tropic Bulbs

With these remarkable shrubs, a host of night-flowering bulbs may be planted to add their sweet scents to tropic evenings. The number and variety here is remarkable, for many of the best bulbs for warm climates have night-flowering habits.

Robust lilylike amaryllids of the genus *Crinum* bring to night gardens both spidery and chalice-shaped flowers that appear repeatedly throughout the year following rains. The enormous clusters of blooms open freshly with the dusk and look spectacular under moonlight, providing whirring centers of activity for the hawkmoths. Choice species include *Crinum asiaticum*, with masses of white magnolia-scented stars, *Crinum jagus* 'Rattrayi', with bunched creamy tulip-shaped blooms that smell of vanilla, and *Crinum moorei* v. *schmidtii*, with custard-scented ivory goblets carried elegantly on tall stems. These species are hardy along the Gulf and, like all crinums, grow lustily on rich, moist earth.

Further inland, hybrids like *Crinum* x *powellii* 'Album' and *Crinum* 'White Queen' can be depended upon to flower wherever the ground does not freeze deeply. Best of all for night gardens, however, are the scented cultivars that descend from the native swamp lily, *Crinum americanum*, for these inherit fragrances to rival the finest perfumes of Grasse. The old pink-striped clone called 'Nassau' and the blush colored hybrids, 'Twelve Apostles', 'Alamo Village', and 'Mrs. James Hendry', are all powerfully fragrant. Where frost is

Night jessamine, *Cestrum nocturnum*
(Greg Grant)

Yesterday-today-and-tomorrow, *Brunfelsia
calycina* (Greg Grant)

Lady of the night, *Brunfelsia americana*
(Paul Cox)

Lady of the night orchid, *Brassavola
nodosa*

Cape jasmine, *Gardenia jasminoides*
'Mystery'

not severe, the gigantic Queen Emma Lily (*Crinum × amabile*) may be set out to radiate its wondrous perfume from the lolling stalks of oversized wine-striped spider blossoms that emerge at the sides of its massive leeklike bulbs.

For nocturnal gardens along the Gulf, the essential *Crinum* must be an old clone called the 'Empress of India'. This Victorian flower bears its floppy, wine-striped stars on tall, dusty purple stems. The powerfully fragrant nine-inch flowers can be seen properly only on moon-filled nights, for they fold promptly and wither at dawn. One could hardy ask for a more wonderful inducement to stay out strolling among the evening flowers.

The gossamer petals of the spider lilies (*Hymenocallis* spp.) mark these amaryllids even more clearly than crinums as flowers of evening. Their slim white segments splay outwards in a star pattern, guiding the hawkmoths towards pale, diaphanous cups that join the overly long stamens in the center of the blossoms. As they sip nectar from the deep tubes of the flowers, the moths dislodge gold pollen from anthers that swivel and hang at the ends of the filaments, passing fertile dust to the sticky, gel-tipped pistil.

Several of these nocturnal flowers may be added to garden plantings, all with thin, ghostly blooms and lush fountains of foliage. In order of bloom, *Hymenocallis imperialis*, *H.* 'New Lion', *H. maximiliani*, *H.* 'Tropical Giant', *H. latifolia*, and *H. acutifolia* bring delicious spider blossoms to evenings from May to October, radiating perfumes reminiscent of magnolia, jasmine, and vanilla. Like crinum, these big bulbs thrive on rich soil, warmth, and abundant moisture. The nightly opening of their ethereal blossoms provides some of the most precious moments in any garden under the moon, for no flower is more clearly in sympathy with the evening than the spider lily.

As companions for these, the small nocturnal rain lilies may be set along paths or in the foreground of plantings where the sweet scent of their pale-toned funnels can be inhaled. These night-flowering fairy lilies, sometimes called *Cooperia*, differ from ordinary day-blooming *Zephyranthes* in their long tubes and night fragrance. Under moonlight, the gray-leafed, ivory-blossomed *Zephyranthes drummondii* (*Cooperia pedunculata*) and the sulfury yellow *Zephyranthes smallii* offer rare charms for night gardens. Their sprightly, spontaneous flowers appear sporadically after rains from March through October, opening at dusk to draw the moths near.

Bunches of the like-scented acidanthera (*Gladiolus callianthus*) might also be set in rich, moist soil so that they can add their moth perfume to summer evenings. The sword-shaped leaves of these night-flowering gladiolus provide dark foils for the long-tubed, ivory, brown-eyed blooms. Along with these upright spikes of scented blossoms, several clumps of the irislike fortnight lilies (*Dietes* spp.) might be positioned so their flat orchid-style blooms could catch the moonrays. The yellow African iris (*Dietes bicolor*) sends out primrose, brown-spotted blooms in several crops over summer, multiplying swiftly in ordinary garden soil. On decidedly damp ground, its cousin, the white fortnight lily (*Dietes vegeta*), sends up fleeting showers of larger silkier blooms as silvery as the moon.

The unsurpassed perfume of the tuberose (*Polianthes tuberosa*) might waft over all of this if a little good earth can be found for their clumping root-stocks. The glistening blooms of these old-fashioned bulbs sparkle under moonlight like bone china, filling the night with an overpowering sweetness. To prolong their magical effects, the tubers may be set out at two-week intervals beginning in late spring for bloom in summer and autumn. 'Mexican Single' and 'Double Pearl' are both amazingly sweet; a variegated sport with creamy margins along the spiky leaves might show up well at night.

With these, the supremely sweet torches of the white butterfly gingers (*Hedychium coronarium*) will swallow late summer evenings in romantic perfume. On moist soil, these rampant herbs proliferate, creeping on lusty roots that send up milky, orchidlike blooms with increasing frequency as summer progresses to autumn. As the growing season closes they will be joined by the sweet kahili gingers (*H. gardnerianum*), whose slender-petaled yellow blooms send forth the fragrance of heaven itself.

Trees

Sheltering these rhizomatous perennials, subtropic trees like the mimosa (*Albizia julibrissin*) add their own subtle scents to the night. The blowsy pink powderpuffs of this suburban tree emit a peculiar too-sweet aroma that may be detected even when the trees cannot be seen. When their feathery-leafed branches are spotted under the moon, the leaves of the mimosa will be seen folded, for this is one of the legumes that sleep at night.

The potent chinaberry (*Melia azedarach*) also enriches the scents of subtropic evenings, and its clusters of pale lavender blooms are large enough to show under the spring moons. In fall, the mushroom-shaped canopy carries amber berries that show at night even after the feathery leaves have turned gold and fallen from the branches.

The satiny funnel-shaped blooms of the wild olive (*Cordia bossieri*) offer little noticeable scent, but these exotic-looking trees emit a vague, pleasant fragrance anyway, perhaps from their ripening fruits. In bloom the masses of milky flowers and rough gray leaves provide one of the most arresting sights under the moon. Fat yellowish fruits follow and further enhance the wild olive's value under moonlight. A south Texas native, *Cordia* thrives along the Gulf, enduring drought and poor soil.

The slender spider blossoms of the Brazilian orchid tree (*Bauhinia forficata*) have the aspect of night flowers, although these creamy spring and summer blooms seem to attract butterflies rather than moths. White floss silk trees (*Chorisia insignis*), also from South America, have exotically large blossoms that arrive on their half-naked branches in fall and winter, showing off big bosses of satiny stamens inside whorls of leathery petals. Although freezes damage these trees, they recover and may be planted with success in the lower South.

The tung oil, or varnish trees (*Aleurites fordii*), withstand more severe frosts and have naturalized on the Gulf Coast where they were once planted for oil. Their showy white flowers are large enough to catch the moonrays and result in golf-ball sized fruits that rest among the waxy, heart-shaped leaves. Even more cold resistant, the smooth, pale-green boles of the Chinese parasol tree (*Firmiana simplex*) support canopies of gigantic soft green leaves. These are lobed and folded like the wings of bats and with the tiny yellowish flowers and green-winged seed clusters, show smartly under the summer moons. Although decidedly tropic in its aspect, *Firmiana* is hardy through most of the South.

Palms and Bamboos

As the moon peers from behind the clouds, its cool light might also fall on dark groves of bamboos whose rustling leaves sing to the night breezes. Clumping sorts like *Bambusa multiplex* 'Alphonse Karr', with its thick gold-striped stems, make distinctive accents for small gardens and are hardy in the lower South. Where there is room for running canes to spread, few plants offer more striking architectural forms in moonlight than the henon bamboos (*Phyllostachys nigra* 'Henon'), with robust whitish culms, or the rarer Castillon bamboos (*Phyllostachys bambusoides* 'Castillon'), with yellow canes striped green above the joints. It was for viewing plants such as these that the Chinese built ponds with quiet reflecting waters and gates in the shape of the moon to frame their pictures of tranquillity.

An even more silvery yet equally tropical effect may be had from several gray-leafed palms. Along the Gulf where these treasures are hardy, the Mexican blue palms (*Brahea armata*) grow slowly into noble fifteen-foot trees topped with impressive crowns of silvery fan-shaped fronds. Another Mexican palm, *Brahea decumbens*, and certain silver strains of the native Florida saw palmetto (*Serenoa repens*) develop frosty masses of suckering stems, eventually reaching ten feet or more in height and breadth. The rare Sonoran palmetto (*Sabal uresana*) is another blue fan palm that might be added to gardens in the lower South. With their sweet-scented chartreuse flower panicles, even the ordinary green forms of *Sabal* like the cabbage palm *(Sabal palmetto)* and Bermuda palmetto *(Sabal bermudana)* have much to offer evening plantings and, like bamboos, will rustle in the wind, bringing the property of sound to night gardens.

The soft gray pindo palm *(Butia capitata)* seems most cold tolerant and worthwhile of the feather-leafed palms. It makes a squat tree with a stout stem like an oversized pineapple, carrying fragrant clusters of edible golden dates at various times of the year. A feathery gray Mexican cycad, *Dioon edule,* is another palmlike plant hardy in the lower South. Under the moon, their elegant leafy rosettes add exotic symmetry to the tropic nights.

Creepers

Along with the murmuring tree frogs that chirp from the branches, vining plants might climb into the canopies of trees to seek the moonrays. Sweet-scented Burmese honeysuckles *(Lonicera hidebrandiana)* make lush ropelike vines to carry their slender six- to seven-inch blooms. These tubular flowers open cream, fading to dull orange, and are excellent summertime attractors for hawkmoths. The tender vines grow best with protection from hard freezes.

Rangoon creepers *(Quisqualis indica)* make more resilient performers where frost comes regularly, although they, too, are hardy only along the Gulf. Their clustered tubular blooms fade from cream to maroon over several days, at night sending forth a delicious jasminelike perfume. *Thunbergia fragrans* also lives up to its name only in the evening, for its pristine white flowers are scentless during the day. With massed dark green leaves, its rampant stems make a striking contrast for the flowers, often smothering walls or low fences. The famous moon vine *(Calonyction aculeatum)* is another tropical climber that rambles impressively on rich, moist ground, lifting its long-tubed, white funnels to the moon on summer evenings.

For pots on a terrace, the well-behaved *Stephanotis floribunda* makes a tidy show of waxy white-clustered blooms. Although tender to cold, the sweet blossoms are universal favorites, and the leathery leafed vines make handsome, easily accommodated container subjects. The cruel vine *Araujia sericifera* offers similar night-fragrant blooms and is hardy through the middle South.

Another mannered climber, the potato vine *(Solanum jasminoides)* adorns its leathery green leaves with down-facing clusters of small, white stars. Its yellow-variegated form is particularly showy for evening plantings, providing one of the best of all flowering climbers for shady positions. These are entirely hardy along the Gulf.

Rangoon creeper, *Quisqualis indica*

Banana shrub,
Michelia figo

Hybrid butterfly ginger, *Hedychium coronarium* x *Gardneranum*

Yellow mountain sage, *Salvia madrensis*

Above: A female papaya, *Carica papaya*, in flower

Right: A male papaya, *Carica papaya*

Some of the most bizarre and interesting nocturnal vine flowers belong to certain gourds. The white flowered bottle gourd (*Lagenaria siceraria*), the balsam gourd (*Momordica charantia*), and the dish cloth gourd (*Luffa aegyptiaca*) all are worth planting for their long-tubed white or yellow blossoms, followed by distinctive curved, grooved, or warty fruits. These annuals make a miraculous show under the moon and grow quickly from seeds on poor, dry soils. The yellow butterfly vine (*Mascagnia macroptera*) and light pink Port St. John's creeper (*Podranea ricasoliana*) are other pale vines suited to dry ground. Although day flowering, both make a spectacle in subtropic moonlight, showering evenings with luminous blooms and, in the case of *Mascagnia*, with seed capsules that look like flocks of chartreuse butterflies.

Tropic Perennials

A cousin of the butterfly vine, *Galphimia glauca* makes a handsome shrublet covered all year in small yellow crimped blossoms. With light-toned perennials like white cape plumbago (*Plumbago capensis* 'Alba'), white trailing lantana (*Lantana montevidensis* 'Alba'), and amber butterfly weed (*Asclepias curassavica* 'Aurea'), ever-blooming banks of flowers can be positioned around the garden to catch the moonrays and highlight paths. In autumn, late flowers like the yellow salvia (*Salvia madrensis*) might join this display, thrusting up six-foot stems of branched primrose panicles.

In the subtropics, there are also many gray-leafed plants to highlight the moon. One of the best is the artichoke (*Cynara scolymus*), making three- to four-foot fountains of scalloped, whitened leaves. These gigantic cousins of thistles grow most lustily during fall and winter and should be sheltered from sudden, hard frosts. Rich, moist soil is their preferred substrate, and this suits an equally ornamental cousin, the cardoon (*Cynara cardunculus*). Another cool season grower, the silver dollar gum (*Eucalyptus cinerea*) seems to stand freezes best if it is grown dry but will usually resprout in southern gardens even if killed to the ground. The whitened juvenile foliage of this Australian tree is what most brilliantly catches the moonrays, so the plants should be cut back annually even when not checked by frost.

For bold form, the scalloped, silver-backed leaves of the rice paper plant (*Tetrapanax papyriferus*) have few rivals. At night the tall patches of this half-hardy shrub become mystic forests of dark-shadowed foliage and hoary, suckering stems. Since it has a large taproot the variegated strain of the cassava (*Manihot esculenta*) can recover from hard freezes and will add striking cream-striped foliage to summer displays along the Gulf. A more cold-tender subject, the giant African milkweed (*Calotropis gigantea*) might be experimented with for its weird, pale-lavender star blossoms and whitened shoots of paired, oval foliage. With luck, its inflated seed capsules may even ripen and burst to show their masses of silky seed to the moon.

At the foot of these tall perennials, carpets of sprawling *Callisia fragrans* might hoist their spikes of sweet white blooms over purple-green rosettes. A popular porch plant through most of the South, this easily propagated cousin of wandering Jew is also cultivated in a creamy-variegated strain, a favorite for pots or hanging baskets. Although tender to hard frosts, these succulent herbs and the boldly variegated white spider plant (*Chlorophytum comosum* 'Variegatum') both make suitable ground covers in the lower South, showing dramatically in the moonlight.

Best of all for nocturnal gardens, however, are honest night flowers like the Turk's turban (*Clerodendrum indicum*). The suckering stems of this shrub are whorled with slender leaves and rise to six feet or more by late summer, when the long-tubed creamy blooms begin to open to the dusk. Although native to the wholly tropical Maylay archipelago, like other fragrant night flowers, these grow rampantly in the subtropic southern summer just as in their homeland.

Cacti, Orchids, and Other Tree-Dwellers

Some of the most romantic and celebrated of all the tropical flowers belong to the cacti known popularly as night-blooming cereus. A famous plate in Robert Thornton's *Temple of Flora* fancifully depicts one of these spiny, vining cacti ascending an ivy-covered oak by an English manor house. As the clock atop the tower strikes midnight and the moon peers from behind the clouds the fantastic funnel-shaped bloom of the cactus opens to breathe forth its rich fragrance.

The night-blooming cereus in Thornton's painting is the queen of the night (*Selenicereus grandiflorus*), a tender vine of the Caribbean islands. The name seems well deserved, for in fragrance and beauty there are few flowers more regal under the moon. Huge furry buds appear along the spiny, snakelike stems in summer, swelling over several weeks until they are ready to burst. On the day of flowering, the oblong balls of brownish hair expand, opening at dusk to reveal scaly goblets formed from innumerable amber segments framing the creamy inner petals. A heavenly aroma, something like buttered pecans, signals the hawkmoths to come and dine. Like all the cacti in this group, these enormous flowers will reach perfection by midnight and will have folded by the time dawn breaks.

Most *Selenicereus* need shelter from frost and, except in honestly tropical sections, are best grown in hanging baskets or other containers. A few plants around a patio create a memorable event on the occasional evenings of summer when the oversized blooms appear. In the lower South, one species, *Selenicereus spinulosus*, seems hardy enough to train up a tree or along a fence. Although not so grand as the queen of the night, its three-inch blooms make a good show along snakelike stems, opening their white stars in late spring.

Another somewhat frost-tolerant cactus, *Harrisia bonplandii*, grows from clambering four-angled stems armed like barbed wire, eventually making impenetrable thickets. Although not notably fragrant, its all-white blooms are visions of beauty, ethereal under the moon. Triangle cactus (*Acanthocereus pentagonus*) and snake cactus (*Nyctocereus serpentinus*) are other nocturnal species that grow as masses of spiny stems. Several of the larger columnar cacti, such as the Peruvian apple cactus (*Cereus peruvianus*), also make handsome night flowers. The vining *Hylocereus undatus* is famed for making night-flowering hedges in Hawaii.

The large group of plants called night-blooming cereus actually include several very different types of cacti, but the one best known to gardeners is *Epiphyllum oxypetalum*. This easy, fast-growing houseplant has passed under the name "night-blooming cereus" among generations of gardeners who share cuttings of its leafy green spineless stems. In the summer, several crops of swan-necked buds open along its branches to white, spicily fragrant blooms of incredible waterlily-like beauty. *Epiphyllum strictum* is similar, with starry flowers popular for hanging baskets, and there are several hybrid *Epiphyllum* with softly or brightly colored blooms. In the wild these "orchid cacti" inhabit the mossy branches of trees.

The same habitat suits certain true orchids, a few of which bloom at night. Although they can hardly be considered garden flowers, these epiphytes are actually easy to accommodate if attached to rafts of cork bark or osmunda and may be hung under the trees in summer to share their exotic beauty. The most celebrated of the nocturnal orchids, the lady of the night (*Brassavola nodosa*) makes a small plant with thick, succulent leaves and odd creamy-white spider-blooms of mystic beauty. The sweet fragrance is strongest at night.

There are also several night-fragrant bromeliads that might be hung in the trees just as the orchids and cacti, but to catch the moonrays, the most valuable of all the epiphytes must be the old Spanish moss of the South, *Tillandsia usneoides*. The draping silvery-gray masses of this cousin of pineapples turn the dark canopies of live oaks, cypresses, and other trees into masses of light. Under the moon the mossy, romantically disheveled branches recall the tousled sheets of a bed, a fit background for the liaisons of moths and arboreal flowers.

The Papaya

Like any love, gardens depend on sensitivity and intuition. Nature best reveals her true self to those who listen with whole, careful hearts, enraptured in the rhythms and nuances of creation. Although many times her rituals appear enigmatic, once in a while, especially in the tropics, nature displays herself in clarity. The overt lives of papayas are such affairs, embodying passion and beauty even the darkness of evening cannot hide.

From the moment the black roelike seeds sprout everything about these plants imbues with burning sexuality. The succulent pulpy-stemmed tree known botanically as *Carica papaya* bears its profuse male and female parts distinctively on separate plants—in botanical parlance, a *dioecious* habit. Undeniably animate qualities infuse the plants, which begin their fast-paced lives as tufts of lacy leaves, deeply cut like the many fingered hands of some primordial race. As if destined to be personages of importance, over the course of a single summer the stems of seedlings rise as stately ten-foot columns. The simple unbranched trunks, wantonly draped with potent blooms and voluptuous fruits, support exuberant crowns of foliage that make a pair of papayas seem like two lovers reaching out to embrace.

Under the moon, the male papaya instills the darkness with energy, reflecting silvery beams from his dissected leaves and long streamers of bloom. Like huge creamy yellow jasmines, his five-petaled star blossoms fill summer nights with the fragrance of desire. The female tree holds her larger, waxier flowers closer to her stem, so that the fat succulent fruits that follow build a tower, dressing her trunk like the multiple breasts of an ancient Mediterranean goddess. Under the light of the moon, the whirring hawk-moths keep a constant vigil around the pair, effecting the nightly unions that bring their ambrosial fruits into being.

Except in honestly tropical climates, the cold winds of autumn will shatter these tender plants, cutting them down with the first hard frosts. Still, they may be planted as summer annuals in the southern states and will usually ripen a few fruits before killing frost. It certainly seems worth the small effort required to set out new seedlings each spring. Even in nature, passion so clear as the papaya's is rare, and no garden can have a surplus of love.

. . . and one is glad to reach the dimly luminous
stretch of gravel at the end and hear the familiar
prattle of falling water in the half moon pool. This
is all the sound save now and then the sleepy
twitter of a nestling bird, or from the song
sparrow a sudden silver thread of sound that
cuts the darkness like a falling star.

LOUISE BEEBE WILDER, COLOUR IN MY GARDEN

SIX

The Water Moon

 pool of water offers the simplest magic in a garden. What more amazing sleight of hand than to capture the glowing stars and the shining moon on the rippled surface of darkened waters? What more outlandish floral display than the cupped goblet of a water lily floating on the uncluttered blackness of an evening pond? What more immediate experience of life's abundance than the thronging chorus of toads by the pool, gathered at dusk after a summer thundershower?

Because water is an easily acquired beauty, every garden, no matter how small, can employ it. Even a simple ceramic jar, filled to the brim and planted with lilies or irises, will bring the restfulness and repose of its liquid substance to the living earth. For large ponds, synthetic linings or concrete offer easy construction, or a galvanized stock tank may be set partially into the soil to be surrounded with decorative stonework or plantings. As long as a pond has adequate depth and recirculation from a small pump, it will be almost trouble free. With living plants on its surface and at its margins, a body of water develops a tremendous capacity for self-cleansing.

Since water is the very substance of life, a garden pond reveals itself as a focus of nature's activity. As in other environments, night brings a rich cast of players to the aquatic world. True nocturnal flowers join a varied assemblage of unbridled, luxuriant vegetation in myriad textures and forms. As nymphs of mayflies and darners clamber up the rushes on a summer evening, hatching to fly under the moon, a variety of scenes present themselves to the night.

Sedges, Rushes, Marsh Grasses, and Cattails

Along the edge of a pond emergent plants thrust from the water's surface, creating some of the boldest vignettes in any garden. The ubiquitous cattails (*Typha* spp.), as striking by night as by day, send up their flattened, linear leaves and elevated stalks, brandishing curious fawn-brown seed heads. The unique architecture of these fat cigar-shaped spikes reads powerfully through the darkness.

Typha latifolia, the common cattail of roadside pools and ditches, often seeds itself onto the margins of ponds where it can grow into large, aggressive patches. Nevertheless, the variegated form of this species makes a welcome planting for moonlight. Although equally rampant, the narrow leaf cattail (*Typha angustifolia*) has become popular for garden pools, its slender foliage bringing a unique elegance to plantings as it reaches four to six feet. For a compelling nocturnal scene, pots of this species or of the tiny round-headed dwarf cattail (*T. minima*) might be plunged in the midst of a pool so that their dark silhouettes can be viewed before the open water. All cattails grow rampantly through the summer months, ripening to brownish yellow tones in autumn before dying down to their starchy rhizomes over winter.

Another imposing waterside subject, the southern wild rice (*Zizania aquatica*) forms fans of sword-shaped leaves like gigantic irises. This lush green phalanx of blades rises six feet or more from the water's surface, enclosing even taller stalks that carry the branched heads of seed. Although finely cut, these fruiting spikes capture and reflect the moonrays on translucent stems and bracts, making one of the most visible floral compositions under the moon. The flowering stems appear sporadically from spring through frost, taking several weeks to ripen their edible grain. If planted on damp soil, these seeds will sprout and make full-sized plants in a single season.

Another big grass of the water margin, the common reed (*Phragmites australis*) can become weedy if left to grow unrestrained. Nevertheless, its ten-foot blue-green canes have much to offer nocturnal plantings. The pale blades drape gracefully from the stems to show attractively in the moonlight, and they create a pleasant rustling sound when stirred by the evening breezes. Silky brown tassels of seed heads and yellow foliage in autumn provide further nocturnal attractions.

Like the cattails, bulrushes (*Scirpus* spp.) offer bold silhouettes for the waterside. The southern giant bulrush (*Scirpus californicus*) is particularly architectural, with leafless, rounded stems like six-foot nylon antennae. Certain Japanese varieties have pale-striped variegated stalks. The zebra bulrush (*Scirpus lacustris* var. *tabernaemontana* 'Zebrinus') produces stems in spring periodically interrupted with horizontal bands of ivory. These fade to green as they mature over summer. Its cousin, the striped bulrush (S. *lacustris* var. *tabernaemontana* 'Albescens') variegates its stalks with vertical pencilings of white. These make arresting accents for large water jars on patios, as well as for more sizable aquatic habitats.

Even better in moonlight, the Egyptian paper reed, or papyrus (*Cyperus papyrus*), tops five-foot bulrushlike stalks with gossamer green pompoms. These capture light much like the flowering stems of the wild rice, resembling bursts of fireworks in the night. Since this evergreen perennial is tender to cold, the pots holding the roots should be protected from hard freezes. These sedges are otherwise easy growing and well worth the extra effort required to have them for summer display.

True rushes (*Juncus* spp.) have slender rounded leaves that give them a stiffly upright appearance. Most varieties read as simple black tufts at night, but a few, like the California gray rush (*Juncus patens*), offer pale evergreen leaves to catch the moonrays. These cool-season growers look like three-foot blue-gray shaving brushes when set in the midst of a small pond or at the water's edge.

Like rushes, the caric-sedges come mostly in greens, but a three-foot species of damp bottomlands, *Carex crus-corvi*, is a variety with obviously blue-gray leaves. The odd botanical name of this native wetland species means "raven's claw" and refers to its inconspicuous heads of seed. As ornamentals, these tufted sedges offer silvery evergreen fountains of leaves in discrete clumps. Another gray-leafed native, the Emory sedge (*Carex emoryi*) spreads by vigorous underground runners, making a thick ground cover for a pond's edge. Weeping grassy foliage drapes gracefully into the water so that a patch of this pale species simulates a frost-coated meadow in the moonlight.

Best of all for night displays, the white-topped flowering sedge (*Dichromena latifolia*) ornaments its colonies of lush green foliage with pale-bracketed spikes of bloom. These look vaguely spidery, with a three-sided geometry that shows well at night. The plants remain less than one-foot tall but spread in wide patches if left unrestrained. An ally from the limestone Hill Country of Central Texas, the snow sedge (*D. nivea*) would be good for small ponds or pots, making six-inch clumps dotted with clouds of tiny white stars.

Margin Plants

Although often planted away from water, the exotic maiden grasses of the Orient are at their best as poolside plants and several variegated forms prove ideal for night gardens. The peculiar zebra grass (*Miscanthus sinensis* 'Zebrinus') lights four- to five-foot fountains of arched foliage with horizontal bands of gold like those of the zebra rush. These are even more effective, lasting the whole of the season. Like all Miscanthus, zebra grass revels in abundant moisture, producing luxuriant growth each summer and adding feathery seed plumes in autumn.

Even more luminous, the striped maiden grass (M. sinensis 'Variegatus') erupts in graceful flopping clumps of white-streaked foliage, ideal for reflecting on the surface of a moonlit pond. With abundant moisture, this old Japanese garden plant reaches four to six feet by autumn. An even more robust maiden grass, 'Cabaret' regularly tops six feet. Its junglelike clumps of wide green blades carry strong ribbons of milky white, composing bold pictures of darkness and light. This imposing display harmonizes with the abundance of the waterside, making a noble reflection for a garden pool.

Likewise, the enormous pampas grass (Cortaderia selloana), elsewhere wholly out of scale, seems serenely at home by the water's edge. These well-known, four- to six-foot perennials earn a welcome place in nocturnal plantings for their enormous autumn plumes like pale-feathered torches. Female selections such as 'Compacta' and 'Pumila' offer the best flowers. Variegated strains such as 'Gold Band' and 'Sun Stripe' provide good pale-striped foliage.

For many ponds, the most rewarding edge plants are irises, and for night display few species would be more appropriate than the yellow water iris (Iris pseudacorus), a European species often seen as an escapee on the sides of streams and ponds. Its sword-shaped, upright leaves grow in big clumps like cattails and reach four to six feet, providing a dark backdrop for spikes of light yellow blooms in April. These flowers have an orchidlike appearance that shows attractively in moonlight. The show-stopping variegated form of the species would be especially desirable for nocturnal display as well.

Another beautiful variegation appears on the sweet flag (Acorus calamus 'Variegatus'), a plant with foliage similar to this iris. The flowers of the sweet flag are small and unremarkable, but the variegated sweet flag provides a memorable nocturnal vision, thrusting from the water of a pond with tufts of milk-striped swords three- to four-feet tall. The spreading rhizomes of this hardy bog plant grow easily in pots of soil just submerged beneath the water.

Several other marginal aquatics can be used to add interest and texture to the night. The small white-dusted lavender blooms of the water canna (Thalia dealbata) hang from slender arched stems held four feet above the water line like exotic fishing poles. Spoon-shaped leaves assemble in elegant clusters beneath these spikes to make dark two- to three-foot masses, contrasting with the hoary blossoms. This native wetland perennial is a distant cousin of the exotic Calathea.

The true aquatic Canna flaccida makes striking poolside colonies, as well. The wild form of this native southern species produces small pale-yellow flowers that show in summer above its six-foot clumps of broad blue-gray leaves. A series of "orchid-flowered" hybrids of this species was developed at Longwood Gardens and includes other water-lovers; a pale apricot-yellow, 'Erebus', is particularly beautiful for night plantings.

On a smaller scale, the paddle- or lance-shaped leaves of the arrowheads, or duck potatoes (*Sagittaria* spp.), reiterate a cannalike theme, hoisting clusters of snowy, three-petaled blossoms. Most of these hardy aquatic perennials remain under two-feet tall, dying down to starchy tubers over winter. The innumerable species can be difficult to distinguish, but all are worthwhile for their showy, freely produced flowers.

Although at night they present only simple, darkened masses, the coarse twelve-inch leaves of the hoja santa (*Piper auritum*) are bold enough to show under the moon, furnishing lush colonies up to six-feet tall. If crushed, this unique heart-shaped foliage emits a strong sassafras aroma. A native southern aquatic, the lizard's tail (*Saururus cernuus*) belongs to the same family and makes smaller masses of low foliage with the scent of black pepper.

Against this dark herbage, large pale flowers like those of the pale pink rose-mallow (*Hibiscus grandiflorus*) stand out boldly, complemented as well by their own coarse, gray-felted leaves. The ten-inch blooms of this species have a slight fragrance. Halberd leaf mallow (*H. militaris*) is another usefully pale type, with dark green arrowlike leaves and three- to four-inch white or light-pink blossoms marked with darker centers. These native perennials can reach six feet in height if given abundant water. The salt marsh mallow (*Kosteletzkya virginica*) is shorter, with two-inch lilac-pink flowers on bushy ever-blooming shrublets. All these mallows are day flowering but retain considerable presence under the moon.

Another sizable flower, the bush morning glory (*Ipomoea fistulosa*) might grow along the pond's edge or, like its nocturnal cousin, the moon vine, directly in the water. Ordinarily a light pinkish-mauve, the white strain of this tender subtropical makes a fine nocturnal accent, even though its large funnel-like blooms fold partially at night. Freezes kill back the six-foot stems, but these tender perennials usually prove root hardy where the ground, or water, does not freeze. Another normally purplish perennial, the Mexican petunia (*Ruellia malacosperma*) also has a white form useful as a summer aquatic.

The showy mounds of the smooth-leafed goldenglow (*Bidens laevis*), a late-flowering aquatic daisy, light the night as effectively as any yellow flower. These dahlialike southern natives have a succulent quality that makes the wide petals especially vibrant in moonlight. The fast-growing patches of sprawling stems reach three feet, offering their flowers along pond margins from July till frost.

Other aquatic members of the daisy tribe offer smaller frothier blooms. The marsh fleabane (*Erigeron odorata*), an annual with pink powder-puff blosstems on leafy stems, and white boneset (*Eupatorium serotinum*), a perennial with fragrant white flower heads like an ageratum, are both notable for waterside plantings.

Taller and more finely textured, the seep-willow (*Baccharis glutinosa*) becomes a nocturnal blaze in autumn when its tiny white daisy-blooms turn to silky heads of seed. These last for many weeks, reflecting moonrays like gossamer spider webs. The fast-growing bushes grow to ten feet, making bold, upright masses.

Of similar character, Mexican devilweed (*Erigeron ortegae*) spreads colonies of near leafless whisk-broomlike stems at the water's margin. Fall brings tiny lavender-white daisies and seeds similar to the dandelion's, making an intriguing night display. These robust evergreen perennials reach four to six feet and seem to thrive as well with drought as with aquatic conditions.

More honest waterside shrubs like the elderberry (*Sambucus canadensis*) also warrant consideration for the night displays, as their flat white panicles and slick, divided leaves show clearly under the moon. The suckering shrubs quickly reach six feet or more.

Another woody waterside subject, the buttonbush (*Cephalanthus occidentalis*) maintains a mangrovelike stance, often growing in multirooted clumps in shallow water. Lush green whorled leaves line its stems and foil odd spheres of creamy blossoms. These pale orbs are born at the ends on the stems over summer, sending out a rich, honeylike fragrance. The deciduous leaves of these hardy six-foot shrubs turn a showy yellow in fall.

Bog Flowers

Some of the more exotic flowers of bogs may be grown as aquatics, either in barely submerged pots or the shallows at the water's margin. Of these, the most amazing are some of the carnivorous pitcher plants (*Sarracenia* spp.). These native American perennials occur in damp, acid soils of the Southeast but seem to adapt readily to ordinary aquatic culture. Their twelve- to eighteen-inch fluted leaves hold fluids that capture and digest unwary insects. The pale, funnel-shaped foliage of the white trumpet-pitcher (*Sarracenia leucophylla*) displays darker veins, making an arresting moonlight display. Yellow pitcher plant (*S. flava*) is also striking at night, making patches of leathery chartreuse-toned funnels. Both species also produce strange round-headed flowers of an ethereal pale green.

Equally ghostly, the white fringed orchid (*Habenaria leucophaea*) offers spring displays of bearded blossoms born in compact clusters. These long-tubed flowers are true night blossoms geared to the requirements of moths. Several other bearded *Habenaria* varieties seem to pursue nocturnal

Buttonbush,
Cephalanthus occidentalis

A giant water lily, *Victoria* x 'Longwood'

A night-blooming
water lily, *Nymphaea*
'Red Flare'

pollinators as well. Nearly all the members of this group grow in acid bogs like the pitcher plants.

Another wetland orchid, the nodding ladies tresses (*Spiranthes cernua*) offers fragrant spikes of white flowers. Although slender and small, these colonial orchids grow easily on damp soil, and their tiny white flowers are quite visible in moonlight, appearing in summer and autumn.

More exotic and showy than these orchids, however, are the sweet-scented blossoms of the native spider lilies (*Hymenocallis* spp.), many of which grow as true aquatics. One of the best garden species, *Hymenocallis liriosme*, begins blooming in March. Its distinctive blossoms expand six slender white petals around a delicately frilled white cup, barely colored with yellow-green at the throat of the long tubes. These large nocturnal blooms open at dusk, sending out a powerful fragrance reminiscent of an Easter lily.

The black-coated bulbs of the spider lilies root deeply in pond muck and succeed anywhere in the South if given ample moisture through spring and summer. Their swordlike clumps of dark-green leaves die down in winter but emerge each spring along with the spidery blooms, eventually reaching three feet. The snowy blooms make fine complements to the yellow water iris, blooming at the same time and often repeating sporadically through the summer.

Another showy spider lily, *H. coronaria*, creates an annual floral event in early summer with its ruffled, fragrant blooms. This species comes from clear flowing streams in the Southeast and performs best in acid soil regions. Two dwarf Florida spider lilies, *H. floridana* and *H. traubii*, are less particular, offering small clusters of blooms with lovely, fringed funnel-shaped cups. These miniature night flowers are delightfully scented, flowering in late spring.

Several of the more tropical spider lilies can also be grown as aquatics, blooming through summer and autumn. The narrow-leafed *H. riparia* and *H. acutifolia* from Mexico are both happy as pond plants, proving hardy through the middle South. Their exotic, frilled flowers appear in June and September, respectively, adding their sweet scents and graceful drooping petals to the night. Although rather tender, the variegated form of *Hymenocallis latifolia* makes a striking foliage accent for a pond.

Another bog flower, the swamp lily (*Crinum americanum*) offers the most delectable perfume of any nocturnal aquatic. Under the moon, its slender white blossoms are nearly as spidery in appearance as the blooms of *Hymenocallis*, expanding in compact umbels of four to eight on late summer evenings. Wine-tinted stamens tipped in gold pollen accent the pale petals, appearing like dark whiskers in the moonlight.

These stoloniferous bulbs quickly fill pots and can make large, leafy

patches along the edge of ponds. Although the native *Crinum americanum* seldom strays from water, its close cousin, the South American *C. erubescens*,
will happily spread into the lawn. Since this similar bulb frequently passes as
C. americanum in the garden trade, it is a good precaution to restrain these
swamp lilies in pots or beds with an underground barrier. A miniature strain of
C. erubescens from the West Indies also travels underground. Patches of this
tiny crinum resemble clumps of spidery white rain lilies, thriving when
planted as aquatics. All of these are hardy through the middle South.

Along the Gulf, some of the more architectural crinum, like the
Australian *C. pedunculatum*, make useful pond subjects. The stiff, upright
leaves of this water-loving variety stand up like a bold yucca, providing
dark foils for the spidery white flowers. These appear in large clusters in
early summer. The leeklike bulbs multiply slowly by fission and may be
planted in submerged pots. Light frost will do no harm to the tender bulbs,
but these plants should be sheltered from prolonged freezes. Most of the
many crinum hybrids may be tried as aquatics as well. Although most do
not require bog culture, many accept it. Nearly all offer fragrant night flowers worthwhile in moonlight.

Another pale bulb, the white rain lily (*Zephyranthes candida*) might be
planted in small pots or allowed to grow along the shore so that its immaculate sheets of bloom could whiten September evenings. This autumnal aquatic
begins blooming with late summer rains, sending up rushlike, dark green
foliage to stand through winter. Each rainstorm from September through
November stirs the bulbs to flower, covering in fluttering white stars. At
night, their platinum brilliance reflects the moon's glow like a beacon.

More subtle effects come from the prostrate rosettes of the golden club
(*Orontium aquaticum*), a thick-rooted aroid with spoon-shaped leaves and
slender blooms like those of a plantain. The bright sulfury flower spikes make
this low-growing aquatic visible at night, in spite of its humble habit. Slightly
showier, the spoon flower (*Peltandra sagittifolia*) guards its flowering spike with
a whitened bract, making a small flower shaped like partly furled napkin.

Although useful for naturalizing, these hardy natives hardly compare
to the iridescent brilliance of their subtropical relation, the calla lily
(*Zantedeschia aethiopica*). This, the most obvious aquatic blossom under the
moon, provides glowing whiteness to rival the lunar sphere. The musk-
sweet fragrance of these open chalices matches the richness of their thick,
creamy substance.

These beautiful perennials withstand modest frosts but are reliably
garden hardy only in the lower South. Their tuberous roots revel in the
black muck of ponds, and it is customary to set them in or near water. This
helps to ward off unusually hard freezes, a useful assist, since the glossy,

arrowheaded foliage grows primarily through the winter. Flowers come in earliest spring, appearing on a succession of three-foot stems, each topped with a showy white spathe around a thick, creamy spadix. For nocturnal plantings, selections like the semi-dwarf florist calla 'Godfrey' and the dwarf calla, or "baby calla" ('Childsiana'), offer elegant night poems of whitened bloom and darkened foliage.

Waterlilies

Just as in daylight, the flowers that most transfix a pond at night belong to waterlilies. These multipetaled goblets, floating magically above the reflective surface of the water, imbue a garden with serenity unapproached by less luxuriant flora. For the nocturnal gardener, it is a joy to discover that these familiar glories belong as much to the night as to the day.

Although the common hardy waterlilies close tightly at sundown, a tropic race of true night bloomers graces moonlit ponds through the entire summer. These amazing flowers descend mostly from two exotic species, the Indian red waterlily (*Nymphaea rubra*) and the Egyptian water lily (*N. lotus*). Another rare night bloomer, the Australian *Nymphaea pubescens* produces flowers that vary from white and pink to rose-red. Like other tropical lilies, these night-flowering species hoist big blooms on short stems above the water's surface. Blunt petals and clustered yellow stamens give these flowers a magnolialike aspect also recalled by their sweet night fragrances. As true nocturnal blossoms, they open at dusk, closing partially the following morning, although each flower may last up to three days.

Water gardeners usually cultivate named hybrids rather than the wild species. For moonlit displays, creamy white selections like 'Wood's White Knight' and 'Trudy Slocum' prove superb, with many-petaled blossoms borne in the center of wide green lily pads. Light pink hybrids like 'Texas Shell Pink' are also excellent at night, with seven-inch blooms accented by orange-yellow stamens. The rosy-wine blossoms of popular night bloomers like 'Red Flare', 'Antares', and 'Mrs. John A. Wood' are so darkly toned that they hardly show at night except for their golden centers, and their purplish leaves also recede to blackness. Nevertheless, these types offer a true nocturnal experience and have fragrances as delicious as any night flower. In the lower South, all of these are hardy and may be allowed to remain in ponds over winter.

If a gardener's fortunes permit a truly large pool, the possibility of cultivating one of the giant waterlilies (*Victoria* spp.) may enter into consideration. These primordial plants are equipped with enormous pads studded on the underside with patterned prickles. Their soft-petaled blooms float at the water's surface amid the formidable foliage, unfolding at night in luxuriant whiteness to send a sweet custard aroma floating across the pond. By morning, the spent blooms begin to blush and fade, turning to a wanton purple by their second day.

The best of these fragrant giants for garden pools are the relatively modest *Victoria Cruziana* and its hybrid 'Longwood', because these are not as demanding as the largest of the tribe, *Victoria amazonica*. Although tender, these Brazilian flowers grow quickly in summer and are not difficult to maintain in southern gardens.

At the other end of the size scale, the tiny water snowflake (*Nymphoides indica*) might be encouraged to grow in quiet waters where its floating leaves, like miniature lily pads, could send a succession of small five-petaled blooms through the summer. The clear white, one-inch wide flowers have delicately cut margins that give them a magical grace in moonlight. Although these tropical aquatics resemble waterlilies in their foliage, they belong to the gentian family. Water snowflakes grow quickly in warm weather, spreading by runners.

The Lotus

Of all the plants in a pond, however, none seems more in tune with the spirit of a moonlit night than the yellow water lotus. This native American, *Nelumbo lutea*, bears clear sulfur blossoms with a translucence that glows before the darkened waters. The orbicular gray-green leaves thrust up above the water in jostling crowds, carrying netted veins that make them seem like pale maps of the lunar surface. With their surreal pitted seed pods and dramatic texture, these ancient plants dominate the nocturnal landscape, although their pale flowers have no more love for night than for day. It is as if the lotus derives from a moment in time before darkness and light were separated, a place where beauty shone with its own power and sun and moon shared governance rather than vying in daily contest. It is with plants such as this that the ephemeral creative processes of a garden can reveal a glimpse of eternity.

Close your eyes and open them:
There is nobody not even yourself
Whatever is not stone is light

OCTAVIO PAZ

SEVEN

The Desert Moon

eserts seem to be frighteningly careless places. Austere reaches of rock, severe, empty plains, and deep, translucent skies transmit an overpowering sense of nature's ambivalence. Until the cooling safety of dusk arrives each evening, the shadeless sun scatters the dry spirit of the wasteland on the swirling winds, leaving hapless visitors with ill-defined feelings of exposure and loss.

Yet with nightfall, these ambiguous territories reverse their process of dissolution. The moon draws down to the barren landscape as a tangible, redeeming presence. Bursts of heat lightning appear on the horizon, accompanied by the periodic rumblings of distant thunder, mysterious flaps of bat wings, and soft droning songs of lonely male cicadas. Pungent sages and vanilla-scented whitebrush seep from the thorny chaparral, filling the night sky with rich, memorable aromas. As the night invades the senses, even vast spaces become enclosed as surely as if thick adobe walls had risen to surround the desert. Beauty and abundance are here to be experienced and cherished on a human scale.

Agaves

Under the cool light of the moon, much of the drama of a desert garden comes from the strong, even bizarre, forms of plants. Induced by dryness of climate, the leaves of dry-land flora often reduce in size or disappear entirely, leaving thorny, barren stems. Alternatively, foliage enlarges to spiny, succulent, organs, storing water against the omnipresent threat of drought. Under the silvery moonrays the fantastic forms of xerophytic greenery create an otherworldly terrain. The undisputed queens of this surreal moonscape may be found among the magueys, or century plants (*Agave* spp.).

The tough, mostly gray rosettes of *Agave* glow through the darkness like few other plants. Their massive swirls of thorn-edged leaves often exceed six feet in diameter, resembling gigantic lily blossoms sprouting from the earth. This striking form reflects the peculiar life of these succulent multi-annuals, who, after many seasons of slow, steady growth, end their careers in an orgasm of floral glory.

Most *Agave* require ten to twenty years to mature and bloom, not so long as implied by the common name "century plant," which references this once-fruiting, or *monocarpic*, lifestyle. When a mature *Agave* comes into flower, it is a spectacular, ephemeral moment for the garden. Over a few weeks of spring, the asparaguslike bloomstalk rises ten feet or more, expanding majestic, symmetrically tiered plates to carry the upright, tubular flowers through summer. In the Southwest, the mostly yellowish blossoms of the magueys attract nectar-feeding bats, as well as hummingbirds and various insects. At night, these branched candelabra of nectar-rich bloom suggest the ruined skeletons of an elderly spruce forest after a fire.

Although magueys grow readily from the thin, black seeds that fill their three-sided capsules, most *Agave* also propagate from suckers, which appear at the base of the mature rosettes. Larger century plants usually offset slowly, but some small species spread aggressively and should be planted with caution. Since many *Agaves* are cruelly thorny, in nocturnal gardens they should be sited where they can be appreciated without presenting undue hazard.

The most familiar of the clan, *Agave americana*, is also one of the largest and most cold hardy, with sprawling, wide-open rosettes that stand temperatures as low as fifteen degrees F. The beautiful variegated forms of this ordinarily gray species are somewhat less hardy, but 'Marginata', with recurving, yellow-edged foliage, and 'Medio-picta', with dark gray leaves striped in alabaster, are arresting at night. The nearly thornless A. *weberi*, the dark green A. *salmiana*, and the sinuous gray A. *scabra* are other large species that stand frost. Set near masonry walls or in the midst of feathery brush or open groves of trees, these massive succulents will dominate a nocturnal composition. Although tender to cold, the gilded, fountainlike rosettes of A. *desmettiana* 'Variegata' would be worth adding to pots on a moonlit patio.

Robustly thorny, patterned leaves unfold from the ashen rosettes of *Agave colorata*, a half-hardy variety from the mountains of Sonora, Mexico. As this species grows, its new leaves make bold imprints on the older foliage, creating serrated designs on the living canvas of the rosette. Even at night, these whitened markings remain visible, adding a peculiar beauty to the shadowy landscape. This leaf-printing can be seen in many *Agave* species but is especially pronounced in this variety.

Where hard freezes or light snows appear with regularity, the New

Mexico century plant (*A. neomexicana*) proves a sturdy subject, forming compact three- to four-foot rosettes of dusty gray, black-spined leaves. These solitary plants resemble large silvery artichokes and seem to grow equally well in sun or shade, offsetting slowly or not at all. *A. havardiana* and A. *Parryi* are similar. All withstand temperatures near zero degrees F. Their rotund gray rosettes are at their best on winter nights when they are crisply lined in frost.

Many of the small *Agave* species send up simple cylindrical spikes of bloom instead of the branched stalks seen in the large forms. These mostly yellow-green flowers appear freely, for the small magueys often grow in clumps. *Agave striata*, a hardy, sun-loving dwarf with silvery-gray tufts of needlelike leaves, shows especially well under the moon.

Although mostly green, the white-edged leaves of *Agave victoriae-reginae,* and A. *toumeyana* show smartly at night, making these dwarfs especially beautiful. *Agave lophantha* 'Univittata' ornaments its thorny rosettes with pale-green stripes down the center of each leaf, while the nearly spineless A. *bracteosa* and A. *celsii* earn positions in nocturnal designs for their pale chartreuse rosettes. These dwarf species are hardy to near twelve degrees F, growing best in partial shade.

Yucca

Joining the magnificent magueys, their truly nocturnal cousins the yuccas hoist torchlike trusses of white to the desert evenings. Although rarely witnessed in the garden, the partnership of these shrubby lilies with the yucca moth (*Tegeticula yuccasella*) is one of the celebrated associations of plant with insect. The night-flying moths, as white as the pendant bells of the yucca, are the only creatures able to pollinate the flowers of their hosts. In exchange for this service, the moths deposit eggs on the ripening yucca stalk so that their hatching larvae can feed and grow. The plant sacrifices a portion of its developing seed to the insect but ensures survival for itself and for the next generation of moths.

Under the clear rays of the moon, the colossal mountain of flowers produced by the Spanish bayonet (*Yucca treculeana*) offers the most magnificent of the desert's night displays. The unscented bell-shaped blooms assemble in huge branched clusters above the dark green sword-shaped leaves. These succulent masses of white soften the formidably dark armature of the yuccas as if a hundred ivory tulips had been suspended together in a nocturnal bouquet. This species and its western variant, *Y. treculeana* v. *torreyi*, are the most generous of their tribe in bloom, sending up thick flower stalks like oversized pink asparagus early each spring. In time, the plants sucker and branch to form thorny clumps from six- to ten-feet tall. They are hardy to zero degrees F.

Pale leaf yucca, *Yucca pallida*

Flor de San Juan, *Macrosiphonia macrosiphon* (Paul Cox)

Century plant, *Agave americana*

Spanish bayonet, *Yucca treculeana*

A close cousin of these, the massive giant dagger (*Yucca faxoniana*) eventually becomes a small tree of great symmetry and power. Although the plants do not flower every year, when they do bloom they are as spectacular as *Y. treculeana*. As with many yuccas, the blossoms of this species are edible, with a sweet crunchy flavor. The heavy-trunked plants make noble garden accents, withstanding below zero temperatures if dry.

On the low hills where the shaggy-trunked *Yucca rostrata* grows, the passing desert breezes cause its groves to quiver in the moonlight. The needle-thin silvery leaves shimmer as they dance. This rustling is not silent, for the assembled plants send out an unearthly rustling like the trembling of a taught telegraph wire.

Of all the treelike yuccas, this is the most impressive at night, crowning its tawny-thatched trunks with brilliant silver-gray foliage. Since the narrow leaves of *Yucca rostrata* remain flexible, they present little hazard. The shaggy trunks reach ten feet or more and may be left in their handsome native condition or trimmed to reveal the diamond-pattern geometry of the spiraling leaves. When the flowers arrive in late spring, they stand well above the foliage on tall stalks like giant white flames held up to the moon. These shimmering beauties are amazingly hardy, performing well even with subzero frost.

The shrubbier *Yucca thompsoniana* has many of the same talents as *Y. rostrata* but forms branching plants that are not quite so silvery. Soap tree yucca (*Y. elata*), a short-trunked species valuable for its slender-leafed crowns, edges its foliage in white filaments that reflect the moon's rays like satin. The blue-leafed *Yucca rigida* sends up trunks cloaked in bold, stiff foliage, making a dangerously thorny tree to eight-feet tall.

More arresting at night than any of these treelike species, however, are the stemless blue rosettes of the pale-leaf yucca (*Yucca pallida*), a dwarf species from the limestone cedar brakes of North Texas. Its handsomely wide leaves make twelve-inch silver stars on the earth. In May, these send up four- to six-foot stalks of pendulous ivory blooms. Like most yuccas, this hardy species will grow in considerable shade as well as in full sun.

Although not true desert plants, the yuccas of the southeastern coasts, *Yucca gloriosa*, *Y. recurvifolia*, and *Y. aloifolia*, often find their way into dry landscapes, for their native haunts among the dunes have pre-adapted them to drought. These popular garden varieties are free blooming and well suited to the more humid conditions of the Southeast. The Adam's needle (*Yucca filamentosa*) is another easterner that might be planted to bring a desert aesthetic to a moist environment. There are several boldly variegated forms of the species invaluable for night displays.

A Mexican cousin of the yuccas, the samandoque (*Hesperaloe funifera*), blooms at night from stemless clumps of stiff, upright foliage. Its lightly branched ten-foot stalks appear in summer, carrying small, bell-shaped blooms that reflex like small, creamy lilies, opening only at night. When seen in the light of the moon, these waxy flowers sparkle like frost.

H. *funifera* has become a popular garden plant in some parts of the Southwest but is less often seen than its day-flowering cousin, the red yucca (*H. parvifolia*). Nurseries offer a beautiful yellow-flowered form of this normally coral-colored species that would be useful in moonlit displays. These yucca allies are thoroughly hardy and easy growing.

Cacti

Along with *Agave* and *Yucca*, the exotic silhouettes of the cacti have much to offer nocturnal gardens. Hardier prickly pears like the cow-tongue cactus (*Opuntia lindheimeri* v. *linguiformis*), the spineless gray prickly pear (*O. ellisiana*), and the purple prickly pear(*O. violacea* v. *santa-rita*) form especially striking shrubs composed of oddly flattened stems.

The bristling spines of the icicle cactus (*Opuntia tunicata*) make its clumps look like patches of snow on the ground. A golden yellow-spined form, *O. tunicata* v. *davisii*, develops into a small, prickly shrub that shimmers in moonlight. Although beautiful and rather hardy, these "chollas" are vengefully thorny.

The giant cacti of the Southwest, the saguaros (*Carnegiea gigantea*) rarely thrive outside their native range, but where they can be grown, these noble sentinels certainly warrant inclusion in moonlit compositions. Mature saguaros produce nocturnal flowers in summer to attract pollen-feeding bats, and the fat ivory blooms make an extraordinary addition to moonlit plantings.

Another treelike cactus, *Trichocereus terscheckii* is slightly more cold hardy and might be tried more widely in the Southwest. In their native Argentina, these massive plants reach thirty feet and are known as giant cardoons. Their many-petaled white blooms appear at various points along the stems in February.

An unlikely cousin of the saguaro, *Neobuxbaumia polylopha* hails from the oak forests of eastern Mexico, preferring shady conditions over the exposure of the desert sun. Since this species withstands frost and accepts humidity, it is successful in southeastern gardens, proving hardy along the Gulf. Although day blooming, its unbranched columnar stems drape in soft gold spines that glow in the moonrays.

Several Mexican cacti cover themselves so thoroughly in pale hairs and spines that they truly glow at night. The woolly columns of the old man cactus (*Cephalocereus senilis*), the fat cottony stars of the bishop's cap (*Astrophytum myriostigma*), and the whitened balls of *Mammillaria parkinsonii* are favorites. The popular golden barrel (*Echinocactus grusonii*) dresses in translucent yellow spines that shimmer in the moonbeams. All of these have much to offer nocturnal gardens but will need to be kept in pots unless they can be given near frost-free conditions.

Likewise, the desert night-blooming cereus (*Peniocereus greggii*) is a garden plant only for warm deserts. Like its tropical cousins, this is a slender vining cactus, but it differs from its tree-climbing relations by growing from an enlarged, tuberous root. This turnip-shaped tuber usually hides under a thorny bush so that the cactus remains invisible except on the summer evenings when it opens its white chalices. As with other night-flowering cacti, these exotic blooms send out a sweet fragrance on the desert air.

Other Succulents

Where winter temperatures seldom fall below twenty degrees F, succulents in several other families may be added to the night gardens. The swollen gray leaves of the "aloe vera" (*Aloe barbadensis*) swiftly offset to form clumps like a small *Agave*. In late winter, these African lilies send up luminous spikes of tubular, yellow flowers. The soap aloe (*A. saponaria*), with prickly, spotted leaves, offers saffron-toned blooms. Although its foliage is not so striking at night as the aloe vera, its flowers appear at odd moments throughout the year, glowing through the darkness like exotic candelabra. A dwarf relation of these succulents, *Bulbine frutescens* is equally free with its yellow blooms.

The coral-like gray stems of candelilla (*Euphorbia antisyphilitica*) give desert plantings a surreal reeflike aspect, as if the garden had submerged beneath some tropical lagoon. An odd desert milkweed, *Asclepias subulata* makes clumps of slender, snaking stems comparable in their curious rubbery beauty.

Some members of the ice-plant tribe with gray foliage like the half-hardy *Maleophora crocea* might be added to plantings as ground cover. In troughs or raised beds where they can be appreciated, the tiny gray, stonelike succulents, *Stomatium* spp., might be set to show off their truly nocturnal flowers. These miniature South African perennials stand a great deal of frost, opening fragrant creamy-yellow blooms on summer evenings. *Neohenricia sibbettii* is another night bloomer in this group worth growing just for its tiny flowers, which exhale a delicious perfume at dusk. Although less hardy than *Stomatium*, these grow easily and will propagate from short runners.

If kept dry, the hoary gray rosettes of the false agave (*Hechtia scariosa*) stand a good deal of frost and would make handsome clumps in moonlight. These terrestrial bromeliads send up branched stalks of mostly gray flowers in late summer. Another member of the family, *Dyckia*, is also fairly hardy and

Mignonette or Madeira vine, *Anredera cordifolia* (Greg Grant)

Henna or reseda, *Lawsonia inermis* (Greg Grant)

Blue ranger, *Leucophyllum zygophyllum*

Desert jasmine, *Menodora longiflora* (Paul Cox)

Silver ponyfoot, *Dichondra argentea* (Paul Cox)

available in yellow-flowered strains suited for nocturnal displays. Both *Hechtia* and *Dyckia* are thoroughly armed with prickles along their succulent leaves, commanding respect.

Where these thorny rosette plants are too threatening, the American aloes, or rattlesnake plants (*Manfreda* spp.), may be set to form attractive tufts of curiously spotted and mottled foliage. These flaccid succulents are diminutive allies of the century plants ideal for nestling at the foot of desert shrubs or trees. *Manfreda tuberosa*, *M. undulata*, and *M. sileri* are evergreen types with tall spikes of bloom in brown and chartreuse tones. The oddly scented flowers have fragrances suggestive of rubber, and their long protruding stamens give the bloom spikes a bottlebrush effect as they attract hummingbirds and night-flying moths.

A heavily spotted Mexican species distributed under the name 'Maculata Gigantea' runs rampantly on underground stems, dying down with frost like the native Southeastern *Manfreda virginica*. *M. maculosa*, a true night-blooming dwarf from South Texas, forms small rosettes of spotted leaves graced by short spikes of waxy white, sweetly fragrant blooms. All of these are hardy to ten degrees F or less, thriving on dry, gravely soil in sun or shade.

Grass, Bear Grass, and Sotol

When glancing moonbeams strike the softly feathered plumes of the bamboo Muhly grass (*Muhlenbergia dumosa*), they are caught in the gossamer froth of this strange desert grass, creating fountains of light. The half-woody stalks of this unusual species clump to form vase-shaped bunches of fine-cut foliage up to six-feet tall. These leaves remain evergreen to twenty degrees F and bring a lush, ferny look to desert landscapes. Another big desert grass, the sacaton (*Sporobolus wrightii*) earns a place in night gardens for its six-foot knots of strawlike foliage, topped in the fall by airy panicles of seed. Both grasses grow swiftly on dry, gritty soil.

On a smaller scale, tufts of the ruby grasses (*Rhychelytrum neriglume*) might be encouraged to grow in the foreground of plantings so that their blue-gray leaves could pick up the moon's illuminations. The garnet-red spikes of this twelve-inch grass resemble dark flames against its pale foliage. Ruby grass comes from the dry plains of South Africa and grows quickly from seed, proving hardy to twenty degrees F or less.

Many of the grasslike plants of the desert have glossy, wiry leaves that shimmer and reflect moonbeams. Bear grass, or sacahuiste (*Nolina texana*), is a distant cousin of the yuccas that exemplifies this capacity, forming squat tufts like bunches of nylon cord. Fat clusters of tiny white blooms appear in spring among its thick foliage. The deceptively lush-looking plants remain evergreen to below zero cold.

The silvery gray *Nolina nelsonii* and *N. matapensis* make graceful rosettes of flattened blades three feet in diameter. In time, these Mexican species develop short trunks thatched in dead leaves like a yucca. With their lithe, silvery crowns, they are some of the most graceful plants under the moon. Both are hardy to near fifteen degrees F.

The many-leafed rosettes of the sotols (*Dasylirion* spp.) resemble these tree bear grasses but have small, hooked thorns on the leaf margins that give the symmetrical heads of foliage a remarkable sense of definition. The silvery blue *Dasylirion wheeleri* and the dark green *D. texanum* and *D. acrotriche* are all worthwhile in moonlight.

Chaparral

After these bold subjects, a *chaparral* of brush and thorn trees may be employed to provide the balance of structure in desert landscapes. Many drought-loving, woody plants have an airy, insubstantial character. At night, feathery desert legumes like mesquite (*Prosopis* spp.), retama (*Parkinsonia aculeata*), Palo verde (*Cercidium* spp.), and many *Acacia* species appear as gaunt, spreading skeletons, with their small creamy or yellowish blooms dotting the ends of the branches. These trees often fold their fern-like leaves at night, leaving only the honey-sweet scents of their flowers to prove their liveliness.

A few desert legumes, like the viscously thorny blackbrush (*A. rigidula*), the frost sensitive ebony (*Pithecellobium flexicaule*), and the mountain laurel (*Sophora secundiflora*), have lustrous foliage that reads as a mass of black in a moonlit landscape. Nurseries also offer a gray-foliaged strain of the mountain laurel called 'Silver Peso', so these rounded trees appear in both light and dark garden forms. The grape-scented spring flowers of the mountain laurels are a treat. Since these plants grow easily from their reddish, poisonous seeds and withstand fifteen degrees F or less, they may be planted freely in desert gardens to help create a sense of enclosure.

Small trees like the bird of paradise (*Caesalpinia gilliesii*), with its yellow-ish feather-duster blooms, and the Anacacho orchid tree (*Bauhinia lunareoides*), with its clusters of white or pink soft-petaled flowers, are as exotic by night as in the day. The white forms of the desert willow (*Chilopsis linearis*) and the creamy fragrant ash (*Fraxinus cuspidata*) also show boldly in nocturnal schemes, and the ash scents the spring air with a delicious vanilla perfume.

A similar fragrance appears later in summer from the whitebrush (*Aloysia gratissima*), an ambiguous-looking cousin of lantana with small leaves

and tiny white flowers. After summer rains, these inconspicuous blossoms perfume desert evenings for weeks. An unrelated shrub, the kidneywood
(*Eysenhardtia texana*), closely resembles whitebrush in habit, flower, and fragrance. Even more penetrating aromas seep from henna *(Lawsonia inermis)*, a
tender Middle Estern shrub with tiny pale blooms that fill summer nights with
the scent of spiced oranges.

Several dry-land shrubs offer flowers pale enough to show at night. The
white-flowered *Cordia parvifolia*, a Mexican shrub related to the forget-me-
not, and the satiny white Apache plume *(Fallugia paradoxa)* are both excellent
in moonlight, with small, pale blossoms like single dog roses. The Apache
plume follows its flowers with clouds of silky achenes that ripen along the ends
of its stems. When moonbeams strike these feathery seeds, they can illuminate a dry desert wash or a mark a path through the darkness.

Many desert plants assume more or less gray aspects, either from
downy, felted foliage or from honestly blue-toned leaves. At night, these pale
shrubs bring the distant whiteness of the lunar surface down to the earth.
This abundance of light, more than anything else, gives desert gardens their
spirit of openness.

The list of gray bushes available to desert gardeners is nearly limitless.
Four wing salt-bush *(Atriplex canescens)*, winter fat *(Ceratoides lanata)*,
shrubby germander *(T. fruticans)*, and desert-lavender *(Hyptis emoryi)* all
make handsome gray mounds to lighten the desert night, proving hardy over
a wide territory. The *Hyptis* also makes a delightful plant to brush up against,
with soft-felted foliage scented by a patchouli-like fragrance.

Several plants add yellow or orange flowers to their silvery-gray masses,
making intriguing compositions for night gardens. The daisylike *Baileya multi-
radiata*, the ferny *Senna lindheimeriana*, and the frothy gray butterfly bush
(Buddleia marrubifolia) make memorable night scenes, blooming continuously
through the summer. The shrubby Jerusalem sage *(Phlomis fruticosa)* chooses
late spring as its moment of glory, topping its gray-green mounds with whorls
of gold. This Mediterranean subshrub is as striking at night as in the day and
grows easily on dry, well-drained soils, proving hardy to twelve degrees F.

The native barberries, or *agaritas*, of the Southwest *(Berberis trifoliolata*,
B. *haematocarpa*, and B. *swayseyi)* make sturdy evergreens covered in gray-
hued, thorny leaves. Late winter brings a faithful yield of golden flowers followed promptly by abundant orange-red berries. Although slow growing,
these tough natives are hardy and enduring, with a deceptively lush appearance. In the light of the moon, their wickedly spiny leaves resemble jumbled
masses of silver-blue ice crystals.

The undisputed queens of the gray bushes, however, are the Texas sages
(Leucophyllum spp.*)*, shrubby cousins of the snapdragon from the deserts of

Texas and Mexico. Their Spanish name, *ceniza*, means "ashes," and the botanical name, *Leucophyllum*, means "milk-leaf," both referring to their mostly gray, felted foliage. With summer rains, these soft-wooded shrubs add crops of tubular flowers to their dusty, whitened masses. Under the moon, their glistening paleness fills desert landscapes with softness and light.

The wild form of Texas sage (*Leucophyllum frutescens*) usually reaches four to six feet, sprawling gracefully to carry lilac-pink blooms. These appear through the summer months, littering the ground beneath the scraggly bushes as they fade. 'Compacta' and 'Silverado' are dwarf strains that offer lush masses of gray, frothy foliage for hedges or formal plantings. These are hardy to fifteen degrees F or less.

Although the pink bloom of these is pale enough to show at night, 'White Cloud' is even more dramatic, with snowy flowers and especially silvery foliage. The blossoms of 'Convent' are a deep magenta that looks black in the night, but its whitened leaves and loose, open habit make it outstanding for nocturnal plantings. 'Rain Cloud' is worthwhile for its small, silvery foliage and strikingly upright growth.

Monterey sage (*Leucophyllum langmaniae*), a bushy Mexican species, usually grows with largely green foliage, but one of its forms, the everblooming 'San Jose', displays soft lilac blooms against pale gray-green leaves. Other exotic types, like *L. pruinosum* and *L. revolutum*, combine pale foliage with fruity-scented purplish blossoms. Most brilliant of all at night, the blue ranger (*Leucophyllum zygophyllum*) and the silverleaf sage (*L. candidum* 'Silver Cloud') display violet-blue flowers against compact shrublets of titanium whiteness.

Incidentals

Around and among these shrubs, a variety of herbaceous or carpeting plants can be positioned to add detail to the garden. The white tufts of the desert mistflower (*Eupatorium greggii* 'Alba'), the pale brooms of the pink bush penstemon (*Penstemon ambiguus*), and the soft yellow chuparosa, or hummingbird bush (*Justicia californica* 'Aurea'), are all superb in moonlight, flowering continuously through summer. The pale primrose funnels of the desert rose mallow (*Hibiscus coulteri*) offer their sizable blooms over a long season, as well.

The sprawling gray *Acacia redolens* and the pale-foliaged *Vitex rotundifolia* can be harnessed as usefully aggressive ground covers for large areas. For more intimate positions, earth-hugging carpets of snow-leaf sage (*Salvia chionophylla*), silver ponyfoot (*Dichondra argentea*), and a trailing ally of the cenizas, *Leucophyllum tomentosa*, offer pools of gray to catch the moonrays.

With its vetchlike aromatic foliage, the silver carpets of trailing indigo bush (*Dalea greggii*) make especially wonderful cover for nocturnal plantings, thriving on dry, rocky ground. The small shrublets of silver indigo bush (*Dalea bicolor* v. *argyrae*) and the pale yellow-flowered *D. capitata* and *D. lutea* are all good at night, as well.

Other gray-leaved perennials, like the soft copper globe mallow (*Sphaeralcea ambigua*), the light-orange velvet honeysuckle (*Dicliptera suberecta*), and the yellow daisylike brittle bush (*Encelia farinosa*), have flowers pale enough to show at night. Although its white funnels close partially during the evening, the silky gray Mediterranean bindweed (*Convolvulus cneorum*) still earns a place for its silver leaves. Even desert ferns like the rock brake (*Pellaea ovata*), the hairy lip fern (*Cheilanthes tomentosa*), and the bulb cloak fern (*Notholaena sinuata*) supply a useful grayness. These drought-resistant herbs have the capacity to shrivel when dry, resurrecting and unfurling after summer thundershowers. Their short, tufted fronds show handsomely under the moon when planted at the foot of dark desert boulders.

Of the numerous nocturnal perennials of the desert, the jasminelike *Amsonia palmeri* is especially winning, with long-tubed white trumpets in clusters during early summer. These are muskily fragrant, as are the long, yellow blossoms of *Menodora longiflora*, another desert native. Both of these perennials thrive on dry gravely soils, drawing hawkmoths as surely as the flame of a candle.

Some of the night flowers of the desert seem to lack fragrance. The angel's trumpet (*Acleisanthes longiflora*) is one of these. This cousin of four o'clocks makes grayish mats of slick foliage dotted in summer with creamy tubular blossoms. The white-flowered wild petunia (*Ruellia nudiflora* v. *metzae*) is also scentless, although its ivory funnels otherwise mimic the fragrant blooms of rain lilies (*Zephyranthes drummondii*), appearing at dusk after summer rains.

The finest scent among the nocturnal blooms of the desert belongs to one of the periwinkles, the flor de San Juan (*Macrosiphonia macrosiphon*). This night-flowering cousin of *Mandevilla* forms colonies of short grayish stems on rocky soil, producing white pinwheels with the heady perfume of a frangipani in summer. Although exotic in aspect, the plants prove hardy to fifteen degrees F.

Several of the evening primroses call the desert home. The pale yellow square-bud primrose (*Calylophus hartwegii*) suckers to form bushy clumps of willowy foliage that stay attractively compact and low, producing large, primrose flowers on summer evenings. Baja primrose (*Oenothera stubbei*) creeps aggressively to form low carpets, useful as a small-scale ground cover. Its dark green mats, dotted with two-inch, lemon yellow funnels, show dramatically under the moonlight.

Surprises among the night flowers of dry regions include bulbs like the white-flowered Mexican star (*Milla biflora*) and rocket, or arugula (*Eruca sativa*), a familiar salad herb from the mustard family. *Milla* is a true desert flower that sends up onionlike leaves and stems of waxy six-petaled blooms scented like jasmine. Arugula grows as a winter annual, bolting in spring to display odd, four-petaled blossoms like a stock. These are a dull yellow color marked with purplish veins, but they show up at night as pale cream. Arugula is self-seeding and can be naturalized along with old-fashioned petunias among the desert brush.

Silk Vines, Madeira Vines, and Tree Tobaccos

Some shelter from the desert sun is desirable even in plantings dedicated to the moon, so a few hardy vines will be welcome. The most robust of all climbers for dry, desert soils is a strange plant called the Grecian silk vine (*Periploca graeca*). A native of the eastern Mediterranean with dark, coarse-textured leaves, the greenish-cream flowers of this climber resemble the blossoms of a milkweed and follow with fruits that split to reveal silky masses of fiber. In late autumn and winter, these silky pods open to the moonrays, gradually drifting apart to carry the tiny seeds off on the wind. Grecian silk vine will quickly overpower a sizable arbor and soon suckers to form a forest of stems.

Another robust desert climber, the succulent-leafed Madeira vine (*Anredera cordifolia*) has long been popular for screening porches. Although the plant reads as a simple mass of dark foliage, the inconspicuous flowers emit a sweet fragrance at night. The vining stems make a thick summer cover, dying down to tuberous roots for winter rest. Like the Grecian silk vine, this strange climber thrives on heat and drought.

Most curious of all is the tree tobacco (*Nicotiana arborea*), a gigantic relation of the bedding tobaccos of flower gardens. Its tall stems, up to ten feet, branch sparingly, carrying large paddle-shaped leaves. These are slick and gray, providing a handsome backdrop for the tubular blooms, waxy yellow and born at the ends of the branches. At night, this nocturnal giant has a pleasantly rubbery aspect. Like many other desert plants, the tree tobacco seems to thrive on abuse, growing especially well in the crevices between paving stones or in the dry earth at the base of boulders. With plants such as this, sympathetic to both the challenging climate of the desert and to the surreal landscape wrought by the moon, a nocturnal garden in dry territory can be a wonderland.

Then come bosky and watery glens, spanned by
bridges, then labyrinthine windings among and
around hills partly planted with the maguey, partly
wooded, then grades laid above dark canyons
and overhung with dark forests of fir, till finally
through a wild, rocky gorge, beside a noisy stream,
we come out upon the plain of Salazar, a green
mountain meadow spread out broad before
the lap of the summit knobs.

CYRUS GUERNSEY PRINGLE, FROM AROUND TOLUCA

EIGHT

The Mountain Moon

he most potent feature in a landscape is often the earth herself. Even in the half-light of the moon, the soulful terrain of a mountainous territory conveys this sense. The thin veneer of rocky soil, sparely dressed with tenacious plants, reveals through shadowy draws and open hillsides the very essences of the earth. Gardens composed on such themes offer uncannily moving experiences and recite unmatched poetry at night.

The love felt for alpine meadows has inspired many gardeners to plant rockeries in imitation. Flora in such compositions often seems to shrink to mere tufts and carpets. This montane aesthetic plays upon a marvel described by the Swiss botanist Claude Favarger in which "the plant becomes reduced to the blossom, and thus becomes the flower in the triumph of its beauty." It is this manipulation of scale, creating illusions of a larger space, that exerts such a powerful tug on the hearts of gardeners. The capacity to lose oneself in a small planted portion of the earth rises as its components shrink.

Constructing a rockery is a simple matter of bringing in loose, rocky fill or base material. This can be mounded attractively and then veneered with well-chosen stones or boulders to suggest natural ledging. A gritty soil composed of compost, ordinary garden earth, and crushed or decomposed granite in equal parts may then be distributed shallowly over the fill. Topped with a scree of crushed stone or grit, this will accommodate most types of plantings. As easy as such a garden is to construct, even such raised beds are not essential, for less grandiose wall plantings, crevice gardens between flag-stone paving, or trough collections of miniatures will all convey the spirit of the mountainside.

Conifers

One of the favorite groups of plants for rockeries has long been the coniferous evergreens. These fine-textured plants read in landscapes as masses of foliage so that it becomes difficult to judge their actual size. An entire race of dwarf conifers has become popular precisely for this character, and with ledges of rock or stacked boulders may be used to suggest the illusion of a miniature pine forest along a mountainous escarpment. Larger evergreens can be just as effective for visual trickery, with conical growth suggestive of the mountains themselves. Under the moon, their varied tones of green and blue-gray provide gardens with shadings from silver to charcoal.

Cold-loving evergreens such as the Colorado blue spruce (*Picea pungens*) generally struggle in high summer heat but may succeed if offered deep, moist, gravely root runs. Their silvery needles seem to be eternally dressed in snow. An especially vigorous cultivar worth trying from the middle South northwards is 'Foxtail', a variety that matures as a narrowly upright silver-blue pyramid.

Deodar cedars (*Cedrus Deodara*) are more at home in southern climates, making graceful, majestic trees with whorled needles and up-facing cones. Their soft, gray-green foliage reminds gardeners of fir. Blue Atlas cedar (*C. atlantica* 'Glauca') is an even more silvery conifer, ideal for moonlight plantings, slower growing and more readily managed than the deodar. An exotic subtropical, the China fir (*Cunninghamia lanceolata*) provides oddly tiered branches of primordial, reptilian character. The blue-gray form, 'Glauca', makes a worthwhile evergreen for southern plantings, developing bushy pyramids to twenty feet.

The scaly, tightly appressed leaves of junipers and cypresses give these hardy conifers special beauty in moonlight and also impart great drought resistance. Most thrive on gravely upland soils with fast drainage. Although most popular in cold climates, several adapt to warmer, more humid sections.

Arizona cypress (*Cupressus glabra*), one of the most striking plants in moonlight, offers beautiful silvery foliage in compact pyramids up to twenty-feet tall. Bluish wax secreted by glands on its turpentine-scented leaves gives this southwestern evergreen a blue-gray sheen. 'Silver Smoke' and 'Carolina Sapphire' are fine cultivars for tall background plantings. 'Blue Ice' grows more slowly, providing a telling steely cone unmatched by any conifer adapted to warm climates.

Another grayish tree, the silver cedar (*Juniperus virginiana* 'Glauca') grows as a wide mass of upswept whitened branches. Although less suited to southern humidity, forms of Rocky Mountain juniper (*Juniperus scopulorum*) make compelling, pale columns. 'Pathfinder', 'Moonglow', and 'Wichita Blue' grow as dense pyramids ten- to fifteen-feet tall, at night forming sparkling palisades of silver. Along with these upright growers, shrublets like the tousled *Juniperus squamata* 'Blue Star' and the many dwarf false cypresses (*Chamaecyparis* spp.) provide the sense of a miniature landscape.

Spreading junipers are the most suitable types for smaller rockeries, thriving in raised beds filled with fast-draining soil. Their low, mossy growth and gracefully sprawling habits complement carefully positioned boulders or stone ledgework and show handsomely in beds dressed in screes of crushed stone. The soft blue-gray J. *horizontalis* 'Blue Chip' makes a thoroughly prostrate shrub, flowing over the ground in a dense sea of gray. Blue shore juniper (J. *conferta* 'Blue Pacific') provides trailing masses of needlelike branchlets. This prickly foliage carries streakings of silvery wax on the undersides and reflects moonrays like sheets of blue ice crystals.

Special Accents

After rockwork and background plantings have roughed in the landscape, textural plants can be placed to enliven the rockery. Some of the most fascinating for moonlit plantings may be found among the perennial spurges (*Euphorbia* spp.). These leathery evergreens cover their shrubby or trailing stems with whorled gray-green foliage. Clustered, mostly chartreuse blooms appear at the ends of the stems in late winter, creating a subtle glow in the darkness. Like other Mediterranean plants, the drought-loving spurges dislike excessive summer humidity but are otherwise fairly easy growing. The upright *Euphorbia rigida* and shrubby E. *characias* v. *wulfenii* make sculptural gray-green shrublets, performing best without summer irrigation. E. *myrsinites* is the variety that grows most easily in warm climates, developing strange, sinuous stems covered in gray, scalelike leaves. At night, a planting on a bank resembles a hillside of writhing reptiles.

A cousin of *Euphorbia*, the sweetly fragrant garland flower (*Daphne cneorum*) also makes an interesting rockery shrub, with clusters of four-petaled, scented blooms in early spring. Like other daphnes, this procumbent Mediterranean species can be temperamental, but a well-drained position in part shade will usually accommodate it for several seasons. Commonly rosy pink, a white variant of the species may also be had. With its pale blooms and dark, waxy-leafed stems, it makes a powerful silhouette in moonlight.

A sturdy western shrub, the mountain mahogany (*Cercocarpus montanus*)

Hen and chicks, *Echeveria runyonii*

Ghost plant,
*Graptopetalum
paraguayense*

Palmer's stonecrop, *Sedum palmeri*

provides an intriguing specimen for sunny crags. Although large for a rockery at six feet or more, this leathery evergreen has a valuable sculptural appearance. The tiny spring flowers are all but invisible, but the silky achenes that follow give a silvery sheen to these plants all summer. Their frothy whiteness in moonlight provides a soft contrast to ruggedly dark stones or boulders.

More practical for small rockeries, the low-growing rosettes of the sea kale (*Crambe maritima*) stand out in the evening like beacons. The handsome scalloped leaves of this perennial cabbage are covered in a blue powder that makes them especially bright. On their native European sea coasts, *Crambe* grows in sandy soils with fast drainage, luxuriating in cool marine breezes. In warm climates, a position at the foot of a north facing boulder will offer a cool root run and some welcome shading from summer heat.

For moonlit plantings, the most appropriate rockery rosettes remain among the mulleins (*Verbascum* spp.), whose felted leaves bolt to bear spikes of soft-petaled, orchidlike blossoms. In addition to common mullein (*Verbascum thapsus*), the silvery *V. bombyciferum* 'Arctic Summer' offers striking accents for any night planting with bold, woolly rosettes of unparalleled whiteness. The furry bloomstalks, like white candles in the moonlight, reach three to four feet. Although these large-leafed biennials sometimes volunteer in gritty soil, they should be replanted from seed each autumn to guarantee a return.

Succulents

Smaller rosettes like those of the hen and chicks (*Echeveria* spp.) may be encouraged to spread through crevices between stones to add their pale tones as well. Despite subtropical ancestry, several of these quaint Mexican succulents withstand frost. The lavender-dusted *Echeveria lilacina* and the clustering gray-blue *E. Runyonii* both accept twenty degrees F or less, thriving in positions shaded from the western sun. In colder climates, the cobweb houseleek (*Sempervivum arachnoideum*) offers similar charms, with whitened woolly swirls in proliferating clusters. An oriental ally, *Orostachys furusei*, is another beautiful gray rosette succulent hardy to below zero temperatures.

Any of the pale-leafed sedums make fine crevice plants in moonlight, growing rapidly in cool weather. In the warm South, the sprucelike silvery-blue *Sedum reflexum*, with yellow flowers in May, and the soft sage-green *S. potosinum*, with tiny white flowers at the same season, perform successfully, draping over stones and filling spaces between pavers with seas of gray foliage. The variegated strain of *Sedum lineare* is also good, growing rapidly into procumbent mats if given adequate moisture. On shady, north-facing exposures, the half-hardy *Sedum palmeri* provides draping masses of a softly luminous green. This branching sedum covers in orange-yellow blooms in late winter, making pale cascades in the moonlight.

Easiest and most effective of all these succulents, the ghost plant (*Graptopetalum paraguayense*) provides sheets of blue-gray rosettes that decorate the night like bunches of thick-petaled flowers. The actual blooms are small and sedumlike, sprouting from the sides of the rosettes in creamy spring panicles. Hardy to fifteen degrees F, the ghost plant propagates from stem or leaf cuttings, thriving on rockery walls or in pots shaded from direct sun.

Herbs

In the South, many of the best rockery subjects reside among the herbs, for these mostly Mediterranean perennials better tolerate heat than actual alpine flowers. *Achillea serbica* is typical of these hearty, drought-loving plants, with spreading gray mats of minutely toothed, paddle-shaped leaves. Dressed occasionally with small clusters of milky flowers, its whitened patches of foliage make effective stand-ins for miniature snow fields on a moonlit hillside.

The partridge feather (*Tanacetum densum* v. *amani*) is even frostier, with filigreed foliage in dense, low tufts. Other good gray shrublets may be had from the lavender cotton (*Santolina chamaecyparissus*) and from the so-called "dusty millers": *Senecio cineraria.*, *S. vira-vira*, and *Centaurea cineraria*. Curry plant (*Helichrysum angustifolium*) makes a useful ever-gray shrublet resembling a silver-leafed rosemary. This southern European native emits a pleasant spicy aroma when rubbed or bruised. Best of all, a silvery horehound (*Ballota pseudodietamus*) makes a luminous soft gray sub-shrub.

Several of the thymes are beautiful in moonlight, making velvety carpets among stones or paving. The woolly thyme (*Thymus pseudolanuginosus*) is especially worthwhile, creeping slowly to form furry white mats. Longwood thyme (*Thymus glabrescens*) and juniper thyme (*T. rigidus*) are others that accept a fair measure of heat and present soft grays to the night. These low evergreen herbs perform best in gritty soils dressed with a screes of gravel or chipped stone.

The narrow, needlelike leaves of silver germander (*T. cossonii*) give this low herb from Majorca a feathery texture in moonlight. In summer, wine-pink flowers dress the ends of its soft gray branchlets. These sprawl pleasantly and smell of pineapple when touched. Even more lovely at night, the Greek germander (*Teucrium aroanium*) ornaments its slowly creeping mats with translucent lavender-white blooms like tiny orchids. These appear at odd seasons all year, looking ghostly against the whitened foliage. Creeping germander (*T. chamaedrys* 'Prostrata') covers in dark foliage that makes the shiny plants look black at night, but its pale pink blooms shine in moonlight.

The ornamental marjorams (*Origanum spp.*) also include several dainty plants for night display. These aromatic perennials were named "Oroo ganeos," or "beauty-of-the-mountain," by the ancient Greeks. Hybrid dittany (*Origanum* x *hybridinum*), one of showiest in moonlight, dresses its prostrate stems in rounded woolly leaves like one of its parents, the famous dittany of Crete, a tender herb with small mats of gray-frosted foliage. Airy sprays of pink-bracted blossoms drape from the plants in summer, flowering for months. These have a papery quality that makes them especially luminous at night.

A similar selection, 'Barbara Tingey', and a marjoram sold as O. *pulchellum* in the trade, but correctly O. *libanoticum*, offer neat, green leaves and long drooping bracts that also show smartly at night. Amaragos dittany (O. *calcaratum*), a hardy species with woolly white leaves in tight mats, gives a white, frosted appearance. The little leaf marjoram (O. *microphyllum*) creates useful gray mounds of tiny leaves ornamented in summer with pale, branched clusters of bloom. Silver oregano (O. x 'Kalitera'), a common culinary variety from Greece, makes upright shrublets covered in glistening silver leaves.

Along with these invaluable aromatic evergreens, the soft gray domes of the dwarf culinary sage (*Salvia officinalis*) will help cloak a rockery in varied masses of foliage like the tapestried slopes of an alpine meadow. With their strong notes of silver and blue-gray, these Mediterranean herbs translate a garden experience to a nocturnal language suited to the moon's pale lighting.

Tufts

In any rockery, the most favored flowers are low-tufting and cushion-forming plants whose full-sized blooms create carpets of color. Although uncommon in warm regions, a few choice types can be found to offer flowers and foliage for moonlight display.

Moss phlox (*Phlox subulata*) is an ideal sort, with clouds of soft five-petaled blooms smothering matted evergreen foliage in early spring. For plantings that will be appreciated in moonlight, one of the white or pale lavender selections can be substituted for the ubiquitously common pink form of the species.

The Serbian bluebell (*Campanula poscharskyana*) is another choice carpeter. Its sprawling mounds of light blue chalices make a show in mid spring. The handsome evergreen plants seem to thrive in both sun and partial shade.

A minute grass, the sheep's fescue (*Festuca amethystina*) makes magical tufts of silver-blue that take on the appearance of tiny gray hedgehogs in the moonlight. These tufted grasses are usefully evergreen, growing best in the cool portions of the year. Tiny whitened flower spikes appear in spring. Another grassy miniature, the blue sedge (*Carex glauca*) forms slowly creeping

A silver mullein, *Verbascum bombyciferum* 'Arctic Summer'

A night-flowering lace pink, *Dianthus noeanus*

Arizona cypress, *Cupressus glabra* 'Blue Ice'

mounds of weeping foliage that make hummocky blue-gray patches in moon-light. Gravely soil and partial shade will help these hardy perennials endure southern summers.

A cousin of the florist's statice, the tiny *Limonium bellidifolium* creates rounded moundlets of oblong leaves bearing papery branched florets in early spring. This Greek species grows quickly from seed planted in gritty soil. Mediterranean cousins, the prickly thrifts (*Acantholimon* spp.) offer unique cushions of hard, spiny gray leaves accented in spring with pink, staticelike blossoms. There are several species worth trying on dry, well-drained sites.

Tufted ever bloomers like the four-nerve daisy (*Hymenoxys scaposa*) make attractive nighttime scenes with their pale yellow blooms born on short, naked stalks. Blackfoot daisy (*Melampodium leucanthemum*) is excellent, too, making miniature shrubs covered all season in white stars.

There are even useful members of the mint family for the nocturnal rockery. The shrubby skullcap (*Scutellaria suffrutescens*) offers low domes smothered periodically through the summer with crops of salvialike blossoms. Although commonly pink-flowered, creamy yellow forms often appear when these plants are raised from seed. This hardy Mexican species thrives on hot, dry sites.

Another Mexican perennial, the velvet creeper (*Tradescantia sillamon-tana*), develops cushions of woolly leaves, filling crevices between stones like lingering patches of snow. Tiny lavender flowers dot the stems in summer, but it is the frothy foliage that makes a show in moonlight. These fast-growing heat lovers propagate swiftly from cuttings.

All of the pinks (*Dianthus* spp.) with gray foliage make good rockery subjects, but the best of this tribe for nocturnal planting is a variety with mats of green needlelike leaves. The sweet-scented *Dianthus noeanus*, a true night flower, sends up long-tubed white blossoms to draw the moths. Feathered petals make these mounded late summer blossoms look like masses of snowflakes and their exotic scent rivals tropic jasmines. From the thinnest screes, nature sends out her nocturnal call of love. With sensuous blooms like these even rocky slopes are not barren under the moon.

But when I try to imagine a faultless love
Or the life to come, what I hear is the murmur
Of underground streams, what I see is a limestone landscape.

W.H. AUDEN, FROM IN PRAISE OF LIMESTONE

NINE

Limestone and Other Illuminations

lthough the living plants in a garden are what most readily touch the heart, the natural structure that frames their view, the underlying skeleton of a planting, can also have a soul. Under the moon, a garden expresses its beauty through the rhythmic patterns of light and shade in its reflecting surfaces. At night, the choice and placement of pale stones can be as powerful and lovely as any planting and may be all that is required to transform ambiguous darkness into a comforting procession of nocturnal experiences. For such purposes, nature has provided a special mineral, a rock that derives from the energies of living things: limestone.

During the chalk age and at other moments of earth's history all the way to the present day, the shelled creatures of the sea have added their substances to the ocean bottom in a steady rain. Over time, their whitened limy remains coalesced to form chalks, limestones, dolomites, and marbles, stones whose natural whiteness reflects the moon as brightly as a candle. The living light of these organic minerals offers a sympathetic glow for nocturnal gardens that can be had from no other stones.

As sedimentary materials, limestones often crop out in layers. These can be broken and fractured to make rough blocks and flags ideal for garden construction. Since limestone is fairly soft and fine grained, it also cuts readily, making one of the best of all building stones. As it ages, the natural whiteness of fresh limestone darkens in beautiful natural patterns. A thin surface coating of manganese is usually responsible for this discoloration. In just a few seasons, it comes to suggest great age. At night, the blotchy mixing of creamy white, soft gray, and dark charcoal seen on an old limestone wall creates a scene as powerful as any vista under the moon.

What sets limy materials wholly apart from other building stones, however, is their remarkable habit of chemical weathering, for just as these sea minerals were born of water, so do they return. The mild carbonic acids produced by thunderstorms cause lime to dissolve, so that weathered boulders take on all the craggy forms that water can produce. Certain reef limestones contain fossils, which upon weathering, dissolve away to leave honeycombed massifs like exotic corals. Redeposited in travertine formations, limestone actually grows like a living plant, forming the stalactites and stalagmites of caverns.

Tai-hu Stones

Breathing spirits seem to inhabit some of these shaped stones. The ancient Chinese garden masters were especially fond of certain honeycombed limestones from Tai-hu lake in Jiang-su and Zhejiang provinces. During the Song and Ming dynasties, many large stones with especially interesting erosional forms were removed to create arrangements in the palaces of southern China. These gardens of stone remain beautiful today hundreds of years after their construction.

The Chinese garden makers used limestones to create natural grottos suggestive of mountain scenes but also selected especially large stones for individual display, usually setting them upright to best show their character. Good stones were selected for slenderness, intriguing folds, hardness, and large numbers of holes. Honeycombed *tai-hu* stones, deeply fissured *ying-shi* stones, and sculpted *lingbi-shi* stones were all revered. Many, including the "four great stones" of Jiangnan, have been given individual names.

With their arrangements of pale, sculptural rocks grouped around reflecting ponds, the old Chinese landscapes possess great beauty when viewed in moonlight. The ancient designers enhanced the night experience further by surrounding their gardens with white masonry walls perforated by patterned windows and circular "moon gates." With graceful, rustling groves of bamboos and plantings of fragrant flowers, these ancient Chinese courts were temples to the serenity of a moonlit evening.

Rooms of Stone

In an idealized Ming-period moon garden, the gentle illumination of stones and whitewashed masonry divides the night into a series of pleasant experiences. As one passes slowly along the edge of the placid pond, paths of pale, cobbled gravels lead through the darkness. Lines of ruggedly weathered boulders loom out of the night to edge the water like gray pieces of the moon. As if entering a new realm, the light-toned paving of the trail might suddenly widen to a broad gravel-topped expanse embraced on one side by miniature outcroppings of limestone boulders. On the other side of this open patio, a bold arrangement of upright stones might stand before thick plantings of dark bamboo. With only these pale rocks to hint at walls, this opening in the darkness has become a comforting room.

The power of these simple white stones to divide garden spaces can be fully appreciated by laying them out on the lawn at night. The human eye is particularly attuned in its peripheral sensibility and will quickly recognize an enclosure when it is on a human scale. The arc of a thirty-foot-diameter circle is about right and can be readily described with a line of limestone blocks, instantly creating a welcoming enclosure. Standing in the center of this circular open space, it becomes easy to imagine the fragrant night plantings that might surround the garden and further reflect moonlight. Entering and leaving the circle gives a sense of passage as the eye moves beyond the whitened arcs of stone.

By mixing gently curved spaces such as this with more linear beds filled with night flowers, a procession of stone-edged garden spaces might be constructed to lead the eye through the night. Pale paving stones, cobbles, or crushed limestone gravels can reiterate the design on the ground and make safe passage through the darkness. As a moon garden is plotted and laid out the observations of the Chinese poet Lin Yutang offer guidance:

> In all arts and industry, all human affairs and relations, the combination of the straight and the curved makes for the best results. In archery, the bow is bent, but the arrow is straight. In a boat, the mast must be straight, while the hook is curved, and in carpentry and masonry, you have to have both the straight guiding T-square and the compass. Sometimes it is better to give a sly hint than straight advice to a friend, and kings and rulers can be made to see your point by a covered, indirect analogy better than by straightforward counsel.

Light in Excess

There is a temptation for gardeners to supplement the natural glow of the moon with more reliable sources of light. Although at first it seems desirable to explore plantings on moonless evenings, there is a price to be paid for this pleasure. Overcoming the natural rhythms of celestial illumination with electrical lighting will set a dangerous precedent. Even when accomplished with sensitivity, this invariably introduces a permanent presence into the night. If one must have a few candles or oil lamps for special occasions, then so be it, but if a garden is truly a love affair with nature, then respect for her occasional privacy is in order. We are better to wander in darkness until the moon wills her return.

In the latter moments of the second millennium, much of our landscape is already too well illuminated. In city gardens, the stars are a memory, lost to the hazy glow of urban sprawl. Streams and rivers, once dark refuges of woodland and meadow, now shine in the night, channeled and cloaked in armorings of artificial limestone, that soulless human rock, concrete.

Yet, in the gentle glow of the moon, the horrors of the present era seem less threatening. It is easier to forget that the earth is disappearing under a sea of roadways, that her bumps and curves are being thoughtlessly straightened, that even her shadowy recesses are being flooded in light. While engineers plot demise, a moment alone with the moon and a few nocturnal flowers can still bring reassurance. The hand of nature is a strong one, stronger than any of the works of man, and if grasped in friendship, it will gladly share its power. In a darkened garden tenderly illuminated by the moon, we can find all our hearts require: a bit of pale stone, a few night flowers, and love.

Resources

The Antique Rose Emporium
Route 5, Box 143
Brenham, TX 77833
(800) 441-0002
Old garden and shrub roses

Buena Creek Gardens
418 Buena Creek Road
San Marcos, CA 92069
(619) 744-2810
Wide selection of perennials

Cordon Bleu Daylilies
P.O. Box 2033
San Marcos, CA 92079–2033
(619) 744-8367
Daylilies

Daffodil Mart
7463 Heath Trail
Gloucester, VA 23061
(800) 255-2852
Wide selection of bulbs

Forest Farm
990 Tetherow Road
Williams, OR 97544-9599
(541) 846-7269
Woody ornamentals & perennials

J.L. Hudson, Seedsman
P.O. Box 1058
Redwood City, CA 94064
Wide and varied list of seeds

Louisiana Nursery
Route 5, Box 43 (Hwy. 182)
Opalousas, LA 70576
(318) 948-3696
Magnolias, daylilies & irises, crinums

Mesa Garden
P.O. Box 72
Belen, NM 87002
(505) 864-3131
Cacti & other succulents

Niche Gardens
1111 Dawson Road
Chapel Hill, NC 27516
(919) 967-0078
Perennials & wildflowers

Old House Gardens
536 Third Street
Ann Arbor, MI 48103-4957
(313) 995-1486
ohg@arrownet.com
Heirloom bulbs

Plant Delights Nursery
9241 Sauls Road
Raleigh, NC 27603
(919) 772-4794
Wide selection of perennials

Plants of the Southwest
930 Baca Street
Santa Fe, NM 87501
(505) 983-1548
*Southwestern wildflowers, native
grasses, & vegetables*

The Plumeria People
910 Leander Drive
Leander, TX 78641
(512) 259-0807
Plumeria and other fragrant tropicals

Rainbow Gardens
144 E. Taylor St.
Vista, CA 92084
*Night-blooming cereus and other jungle
cacti*

Shepherd's Garden Seeds
30 Irene Street
Torrington, CT 06790
(860) 482-3638
Flower & vegetable seeds

Siskiyou Rare Plant Nursery
Dept. 1
2825 Cummings Road
Medford, OR 97501
(503) 772-6846
Rockery plants

Southern Perennials & Herbs
98 Bridges Road
Tylertown, MS 39667-9338
(800) 774-0079
http://www.s-p-h.com/
Perennials, herbs, and wildflowers

Stokes Tropicals
P.O. Box 9868
New Iberia, LA 70562-9868
(800) 624-9706
www. stokestropicals.com
Gingers, plumeria, and other tropicals

White Flower Farm
P.O. Box 50
Litchfield, CT 06759-0050
(800) 503-9624
Perennials & bulbs

Woodlanders
1128 Colleton Avenue
Aiken, SC 29801
(803) 648-7522
*Woody ornamentals, southeastern
native plants*

Yucca-Do Nursery
P.O. Box 450
Waller, TX 77484
(409) 826-4580
yuccado@phoenix.net
*Woody ornamentals, perennials, bulbs,
southwestern natives*

BIBLIOGRAPHY

Adams, William D. *Shrubs and Vines For Southern Landscapes*. Houston: Gulf Publishing Co., 1979.

Bailey, Liberty Hyde and Ethel Joe Bailey. *Hortus Third*. New York: Macmillan Publishing Co., 1976.

Beebe, William. *Nonsuch: Land of Water*. New York: Brewer, Warren & Putnam, 1932.

Berrisford, Judith. *Gardening on Chalk, Lime, and Clay*. London: Faber and Faber, 1978.

Coats, Alice. *Garden Shrubs and Their Histories*. New York: Simon & Schuster, 1992.

Correl, Donovan Stewart and Marshall Conring Johnston. *Manual of the Vascular Plants of Texas*. Richardson: University of Texas at Dallas, 1979.

Davis, Helen Burns. *Life and Work of Cyrus Guernsey Pringle*. Burlington: University of Vermont Press, 1936.

Dirr, Michael. *Manual of Woody Landscape Plants*. Champaign, Illinois: Stipes Publishing Co., 1990.

Eliovson, Sima. *South African Flowers for the Garden*. Cape Town: Howard Timmins, 1957.

Enquist, Marshal. *Wildflowers of the Texas Hill Country*. Austin: Lone Star Botanical, 1987.

Gorer, Richard. *The Development of Garden Flowers*. London: Eyre and Spottiswoode, Ltd., 1970.

Greenlee, John. *The Encyclopedia of Ornamental Grasses*. Emmaus, Pennsylvania: Rodale Press, 1992.

Harrison, Charles R. *Ornamental Conifers*. New York: Macmillan Publishing Co., Inc., 1975.

Johnson, Hugh. *The Principles of Gardening*. New York: Simon and Schuster, 1979.

Lane Publishing. *Sunset Western Garden Book*. Menlo Park: Lane Publishing Co., 1988.

Lawrence, Elizabeth. *The Little Bulbs*. New York: Criterion Books, 1957.

_____. *A Southern Garden*. Chapel Hill, North Carolina: University of North Carolina Press, 1991.

Loewer, Peter. *The Evening Garden*. New York: Macmillan Publishing Company, 1993.

Mathews, F. Schuyler. *Fieldbook of American Wildflowers*. New York: The Knickerbocker Press, 1912.

Mielke, Judy. *Native Plants for Southwestern Landscapes*. Austin, Texas: University of Texas Press, 1993.

Mitchell, Sydney B. *Gardening in California*. New York: Doubleday, Page & Co., 1924.

Nichols, Beverly. *Garden Open Today*. New York: E.P. Dutton & Co., Inc., 1963.

Phillips, Roger and Martyn Rix. *Shrubs*. New York: Random House, 1989.

Robinson, Benjamin Lincoln and Merrit Lyndon Fernald. *Gray's New Manual of Botany*. New York: American Book Company, 1908.

Rollins, Elizabeth D. "Origanum: Beauty of the Mountains." *Pacific Horticulture, Vol. 52, No. 2*, Summer 1991.

Rowley, Gordon. *The Illustrated Encyclopedia of Succulents*. New York: Crown Publishers, Inc., 1978.

Scruggs, Mrs. Gross R. and Margaret Ann Scruggs. *Gardening in the Southwest*. Dallas, Texas: Southwest Press, 1932.

Standley, Paul C. "Trees and Shrubs of Mexico." *Contributions from the United States National Herbarium, Vol. 23*. Washington, D.C.: Government Printing Office, 1920-26.

Stearn, William T. *Stearn's Dictionary of Plant Names for Gardeners*. London: Cassel Publishers, Ltd., 1992.

Stern, Sir Frederick C. *A Chalk Garden*. London: Thomas Nelson and Sons, Ltd., 1960.

Stout, A.B. *Daylilies*. Milwood, New York: Sagapress, Inc., 1986.

Taylor's Guide to Annuals. Boston: Houghton Mifflin Co., 1986.

Thomas, Graham Stuart. *Perennial Garden Plants*. London: J.M. Dent and Sons, Ltd., 1982

Treseder, Neil. *Magnolias*. London: Faber & Faber, 1978.

Welch, William C. *Perennial Garden Color*. Dallas: Taylor Publishing Co., 1989.

Weniger, Del. *The Explorer's Texas*. Austin, Texas: Eakin Press, 1984.

Wilder, Louise Beebe. *Adventures in A Suburban Garden*. New York: Macmillan Publishing Co., 1931.

_____. *The Fragrant Garden*. New York: Macmillan Publishing Co., 1932.

Wills, Mary Motz and Howard S. Irwin. *Roadside Wildflowers of Texas*. Austin, Texas: University of Texas Press, 1969.

Yoshikawa, Isao. *Chinese Gardens*. Tokyo: Graphic-sha Publishing Company, Ltd., 1990.

INDEX